The social history of Canada

MICHAEL BLISS, EDITOR

481888   114

Campbellton N B
        Dec 10 1934

Hon Mr Bennet
    Dear Sir
        Will you please let me know
if the Government voted money for
direct releaf for the unimployed
this winter + who has the
haneling of the money I am an
old man over Sixty I am lame
+ have only one hand I need
help and cannot get any there
if five of us in family rent +
water tapes to pay wood and
provision + clothing to buy + only
my wife to do it all I am unabe to
do any manuel tabor + we want
help + need it bad now Mr Bennett
it was my white that helped to but you
where you are now is there any
thing you can do for me

Cap. Baleau
nov. 9 1934

R. B. Bennett
Ottawa
N.B.

Bur. l'hon. Bennett premier ministre
du Canada. Ses a vous que je doit
ecrire pour que vous, nous donne-
la vie, nous avons rien a mange-
nous avons ete vou. les officier
et le pere des pauvre et il
nous avons refuse de nous donne-
de la nourriture dit nous si
qui a du secours direct j'ai
une grande famille et j'ai rien
a mange et il ont a pas
d'ouvrage par ici pour que
une personne gagne sa vie
aide nous et vous sere aide de

LETTERS TO R. B. BENNETT 1930-1935

The wretched of Canada

EDITED, WITH AN INTRODUCTION BY

L. M. GRAYSON AND MICHAEL BLISS

UNIVERSITY OF TORONTO PRESS

© University of Toronto Press 1971

Toronto and Buffalo

ISBN (casebound) 0-8020-1825-4

ISBN (paperback) 0-8020-6127-3

Microfiche ISBN 0-8020-0145-9

LC 73-163838

Printed in the United States of America

An introduction

BY L. M. GRAYSON AND MICHAEL BLISS

SOME CANADIANS lived well in the 1930s. Prices were very low: by 1933 it took only $3 to buy goods worth $4 in 1926. With bread at about a nickel a loaf, hamburg a dime a pound, a good dress shirt costing about a dollar, suburban brick homes on the market at $4,000 and less, and a thriving market in servants at one or two dollars a day, a family whose head worked steadily at decent wages, say $20-$30 a week, got through the decade rather pleasantly. In fact the average factory worker who kept his job in the 1930s enjoyed a slight increase in his standard of living (though his wages dropped, they did not fall as fast as the cost of living), and the full-time Dominion civil servant actually saw his standard of living rise by 25 per cent between 1926 and 1933.[1] For a few people it was a time to make up the ground lost to inflation in the 1920s, buy that first automobile, hire a cleaning lady one day a week to run the new vacuum cleaner and electric washing-machine, take holidays, and relax in the evenings around the radio. They were the lucky Canadians and this book is not about them.

These letters are the voices of the people who suffered most in the Great Depression of the 1930s – the prairie farmers, the unemployed workers, the aged, the sick, the handicapped, and the very young. These are the Canadians who lived in shacks, and patched their clothes, and hung around the relief offices, and went to bed hungry. And took up old pencils to scratch out their troubles on dirty penny notepaper. And sometimes had to borrow a stamp to send their letters to Mr Bennett in Ottawa. Cries from the heart to the millionaire Prime Minister. If he couldn't end hard times, maybe he could make life a little more bearable with a five-dollar bill or a red wagon. These people, not the comfortable and the satisfied, speak for the 1930s.

1

Had there not been a world economic crisis Canada was still heading for a time of readjustment, perhaps recession and hardship, as the 1920s closed. By the end of that decade the great economic development projects of the first sixty years of Confederation, the first set of 'national policies,' had been concluded. The west was full of homesteaders now, pouring hundreds of millions of bushels of their wheat onto world markets every year. Railways had crossed, recrossed, and recrossed the country; now the costs were being reckoned in the debt load of the sprawling CNR. Railroad presidents, their imaginations frozen about 1905, still preached the gospels of immigration, branch lines, and homesteading. They didn't notice that no one else wanted the immigrants to come because there was no place for them to go.

Fortunately the offspring of the second round of Canadian industrialism had come of age since the First World War. As the western frontier had closed, the new investment frontiers of pulp and paper production, hydro-electric power, mining, and the model-T had kept the economy surging forward. By the late 1920s, though, the first great stages of their development were ending. The pulp and paper industry, for example, was already wallowing in excess capacity and overcapitalization. The auto workers at Oshawa and Windsor were ready to turn out 400,000 cars in 1930, even though Canadians now owned over a million of them and in the best year ever had only bought 260,000. Could the markets for Canadian products continue to expand at home and abroad to absorb the productive capacity of the matured economy? Could more new industrial frontiers be opened up to take up the slack if the old industries had really reached their potential? Would income keep going up to pay the charges on the railway bonds, the hydro debentures, the mortgages, and the bank loans that bought the tractors or the shares in Massey-Harris?

The fact that the federal government found itself in the late 1920s for the first time with nothing much to do but keep house should have been interpreted ominously. But for Mackenzie King the ultimate political satisfaction was to sit watching the nation run itself. Besides, didn't everyone agree with Archibald Blue's forecast in the *Maclean's* of 1 January 1929 that an 'Era of Sustained Prosperity Is Indicated'?

That fall the whole of the western world began finally to suffer the long-term economic consequences of the Great War of 1914-18. Now that the European economies had recovered from the war, there was a worldwide surplus of many primary products, particularly foodstuffs. The smoothly self-adjusting gears of prewar international finance and commerce had never quite meshed again, and the new problems of war debts and reparations compounded the difficulty of restoring the old order. The expansionary, though

reckless, spending and lending practices of the United States hid
these underlying distortions for a few years in the middle of the
decade. But the Wall Street collapse in the autumn of 1929 stripped
away that façade. Two anxious years later the foundations of the
whole temple of world commerce seemed to topple in the
international financial crisis.

Every nation fended for itself in the dark years of the early
thirties. The scramble to protect one's own economy with tariff
barriers, quotas, subsidies, exchange-rate manipulation, and regulation of capital flows, meant that only the most self-sufficient nations
could really profit (though the most self-sufficient of these, the
United States, happened to have the worst domestic problems).
Trading countries like Canada could only lose in an era of unre-
strained economic nationalism. 1932 and 1933 were the worst years
for everyone. By 1937 things were looking up all over the world –
fascism and the threat of war aside – but in North America the
'Roosevelt recession' brought back the breadlines and soup kitchens
and apple stands. Only the coming of war would close them for good.

The Great Depression affected Canada more severely than any
industrial nation except the United States. The causes of the collapse
in the two countries, though, were not the same. The American
economy ground to a halt because of the drying up of investment
opportunities and investor confidence at home; the decline in
international trade only made an already difficult situation worse. In
Canada the virtual disappearance of markets for export staples –
agricultural exports plummetted from $783 million in 1928 to $253
million in 1932, exports of wood products from $289 million to
$131 million[2] – triggered the economic decline. The stagnation of
domestic investment, except in the mining industry (the hungry
nations wanted our gold, not our food), only compounded and
complicated the basic problem. In the farm belts of both countries
the weather turned sour in keeping with the times.

There was a good chance that consistently expansionary government monetary and fiscal policies could have brought the United
States back to reasonable prosperity, and Franklin Roosevelt almost
understood this. In Canada the same policies would have helped, but
by themselves could not have made up for the loss of income from
exports. Because the United States was one of Canada's two most
important trading partners, levels of American domestic recovery

significantly influenced the volume of Canadian trade. The 1930s were a lesson in the vulnerability of an open economy, particularly one specializing in a few staple products, to events outside its borders. There was no such thing as economic independence for the Canadian people.

The economic collapse did not affect all people in society equally. Workers who were able to keep jobs at wages that did not fall faster than the cost of living, investors who held fixed-interest securities or equities in companies able to keep paying dividends, maintained and even increased their standards of living. Most of the burden of hardship was thrown on three major groups in society: farmers, the unemployed, and people coming onto the job market for the first time – and a small fourth group, businessmen and investors who had overextended themselves in the late 1920s or had holdings in enterprises that went down in the storm. Economic disaster, then, cut across normal class lines. Some upper-class people became very poor; many working-class people lost nothing of the little they had to lose.

As a group farmers suffered the greatest loss of income; of these the hardest hit were wheat farmers in the drought-stricken areas of the prairies. The net income from farm operations in Alberta, Saskatchewan, and Manitoba in 1928 had been $363 million. In 1931 it was *minus* $10,728,000.[3] From 1930 through 1940 never less than 10 per cent of the wage-earners in Canada were out of work. In 1933 647,000 of them had no jobs, 26.6 per cent of the non-agricultural work force.[4] Young people leaving school naturally had the greatest difficulty breaking into a labour market in which all jobs were taken and there were more experienced applicants for every new position that did open up. In 1936 the Dominion Bureau of Statistics estimated that two-thirds of each year's 'crop' of young men were unable to find steady work.[5] In many cases the college graduate was little better off than the worker's son quitting school at fifteen. It was a situation not unlike, but much worse than, the early 1970s, and was the first time that Canadian youth began to stay in school longer because there was nothing else to do.

The most revealing statistics measured the numbers of people whose income was too low for them to survive on without public help. In each year from 1933 through 1936 an average of about 12 per cent of the Canadian population received emergency relief. Another 5 per cent of the population normally depended on such existing programs as mother's allowances, old age pensions, charitable aid, etc. In the worst year of the depression about two million Canadians, or one in five of the population, were public dependents.[6] These figures ignore the tens of thousands who were too proud to fall back on 'charity' and the millions whose standards of living fell but not quite far enough to force them onto relief.

2

The course of economic downturns was not predictable. No one in Canada in 1929 or 1930 knew what was to happen to the country in the next ten years. In fact no one in 1929 and 1930 knew what was happening in the country from day to day or month to month because nobody was keeping national statistics on unemployment! Unemployment, after all, did not exist in pre-industrial societies and this was the first major collapse of the new urban-industrial Canadian economy. Lack of knowledge and experience in dealing with industrial depressions impeded every program for recovery or relief. Without too much exaggeration it can be said that the most important 'social work' in the country was going on in the offices of the Dominion Bureau of Statistics, where statisticians churned out the first series of measurements of the state of the nation on which everyone else's judgments would be made.

The federal government guessed, reasonably in view of what the experts were saying, that the economy was only going through a period of readjustment. Such unemployment as there was – Mackenzie King called it 'alleged' unemployment – could be handled as usual by the usual municipal and provincial authorities. King's remark that he would not give 'a five-cent piece' for unemployment relief was a gibe at Conservative provincial governments who also weren't yet aware of a crisis, but it came back to haunt him in the 1930 election, much more effectively than any of his visions. If R. B. Bennett had known what the future would be like, he, too, would have had less to say in the 1930 campaign. His promises to end unemployment in Canada and 'blast a way' into the markets of the world by first raising and then lowering the tariff, or 'perish in the attempt,' were as foolish in their own way as King's evasions. They were more popular with the voters, however, who installed their first millionaire prime minister at the beginning of their worst economic crisis; but they haunted Bennett for the next five years, and haunt his memory in the pages of this book.

Bennett's sharp upward tariff readjustments of 1930 probably did protect jobs in manufacturing industries by forcing consumers to buy Canadian. They also protected the profits of the manufacturers. The national effect of this traditional Conservative response to unemployment was to throw still more of the hardship on the agricultural sector of the economy (in 1931 the price of farm products was 48.4 per cent of 1926 levels, prices of manufactured goods were 69.4 per cent of the 1926 figure; to afford the same quantity of manufactured goods the farmer now had to sell 1.44 times as much produce as he had had to in 1926[7]), as well as encourage more waste and inefficiency in industry. The blasting operation to restore export markets for Canadian primary products was scheduled to take place in 1932 at the Ottawa Imperial Economic Conference. There Bennett faced the moment of truth about protectionism: the interests of farmers and manufacturers could not be harmonized. Forced to choose, he sided, as Conservatives usually did, with the manufacturers. The partial system of imperial preferences established in 1932 had only a modest impact on Canadian exports, while convincing British statesmen of the perfidy of the Canadian prime minister. It was the final bankruptcy of the Conservatives' old National Policy of economic nationalism and the end of their dream of a practical imperialism.

With the Ottawa failure the Bennett government had no ready strategy to promote recovery. The few economists in the western world who had paid attention to the ideas of John Maynard Keynes were beginning to echo his calls for expansionary monetary and fiscal policies to fight unemployment by pumping money into the economy. (The first question always asked about the depression is where the money went; the simple answer is that it was standing still, and the Keynesian method was to get it moving again by government action.) But the numbers of Keynesian economists in Canada were very few indeed; their 'soft-money' allies in the west appeared to be the usual collection of cranks and crackpots. All reformers faced a united phalanx of hard-headed men of business who *knew* that government retrenchment in bad times was the first maxim of Adam Smith, natural law, and common sense. It would be hard for a Canadian government to encourage low interest rates and credit

expansion through expanding the money supply when it had no
central bank to do the job. (Again the lack of preparation – the
banks had weathered every other storm without too much difficulty.
True, their flexibility once again saved the country from the panics
and failures that rocked the United States; but this time it was not
enough.) It would be even more difficult to launch an immediate
large-scale social insurance scheme without any experience in the
field or any technical knowledge of how to make one work. Even if
these policies had been practical the resistance of the investment
community to such seemingly heretical, semi-communist schemes
might well have negated their good effects. Besides, as we have seen,
it was far from clear either that major investment frontiers would
have developed even if money had flowed easily, or that domestic
expansion could make more than a dent in the problem caused by
the export collapse.

As the decade dragged on the climate of opinion would change
and the pressures for action mount. In the short term the best the
federal government could do was vote annual emergency grants to
the provinces to help the unemployed, take *ad hoc* steps of its own
to patch some of the holes in the aid programs, stamp out ruthlessly
any threats to law and order on the part of malcontents and
agitators, and appoint royal commissions and task forces to begin
laying the foundations for further action. Anyway, how could the
depression go on much longer?

3

Taking the nineteenth-century English Poor Law as their model,
Canadians had always made relief of the destitute a municipal
responsibility. Decentralization of relief in the 1930s meant the
most extreme variations from municipality to municipality, urban to
rural areas, and from year to year. There was not even centralization
of information about relief until late in the depression. The situation
was so confused in 1933 that a leading academic expert on relief
found it 'impossible ... to keep in touch with the developments'
because 'there is almost a complete absence of decent official reports
by the Federal or Provincial Governments.'[8] About the only
generalizations that apply to the whole country are that it was
always humiliating to petition for relief and the aid given was usually

not enough to maintain decent standards of living.

Montreal was typical of large cities. The applicant for relief, once he found out where to go (between 1931 and 1937 the relief apparatus was revamped three times), had to present proof of three years' consecutive residence in the city. If he had been absent for any period in this three years he had to prove residence for double the period of his absence prior to the three year requirement but within the past ten years. The applicant had to be employable and was required to declare under oath (*a*) that he was destitute, (*b*) that his relations were unable to support him, (*c*) that all the information on his application was correct. The completed application form was passed on to another office where arrangements were made for an investigator to visit the applicant's home *and* to secure a report from the applicant's last employer. Once the visit had been made and the application approved, the reliefer was given ration cheques at the local relief office for food, fuel, and clothing. His landlord would have to deal directly with the city to collect rent; and the city would pay light and gas bills directly to the utility companies. Everyone a man dealt with knew he was on the dole. And a further check was built into the system by the city's insistence that all companies submit a monthly list of all those hired or fired. Any casual earnings over $3 a week for married men or $1 for a single man were deducted from relief.[9]

In Ontario most relief applicants had to turn in their liquor permits before aid was issued. Usually the telephone had to be disconnected, and licence plates or driver's licence handed in to the municipality to guarantee that the taxpayers' money was not financing the luxury of an automobile. Any undisclosed revenues, or in Saskatchewan assets like a secret hoard of grain, were cause for relief being cut off. Accepting a job, of course, or refusing to accept a suitable job, meant an end to relief. To have purchased beer or liquor in Saskatchewan resulted in the immediate termination of aid, and to make sure that it was not being cheated the Saskatoon Relief Board issued press releases urging citizens to come forward with information on cheating families. As the Bennett letters show there were embittered citizens who needed no urging to inform on reliefers. Perhaps it was because of this bitterness that many of the destitute had to sign agreements to pay back everything they were given. Municipalities at first tried to make able-bodied employables earn their keep; but the supply of leaves, dandelions, cordwood, and post-office sites fell far short of the unemployed's capacity to work.[10]

In 1932 it was calculated that $6-$7 per week was the minimum amount of money needed to provide a well-balanced diet for an Ontario family of five. A survey of relief schedules in cities across Canada found a maximum weekly food budget for a family of five of $7.80, a minimum of $4.10. But it was known that in the small cities of Quebec families of five would receive as little as $3.25 for food relief.[11] The Bennett letters show that the rural situation was difficult everywhere and that some rural municipalities had no money at all for local relief.

Relief agencies paid rent, fuel, utilities, and medical bills with varying degrees of reluctance. At first few municipalities offered clothing relief; gradually and grudgingly allowances had to be made when private charity buckled under the demand. Still, the single most pressing problem of the poor people who wrote to R. B. Bennett seems to have been clothes: it is clear that children were taken out of school in all regions of Canada because they were not decently dressed. Few relief organizations considered that the destitute needed such luxuries as newspapers, tobacco, haircuts, lipstick, or the odd night out at the movies. A common way to guarantee that money was not spent frivolously was to issue vouchers only, no cash. It was not assumed that all reliefers were loafers and cheats, only that tight controls had to be established to stop those who were. The public grudgingly accepted its responsibility for the poor, but only to keep them alive.[12]

Local relief was always confined to people who could prove that they had resided in the area for a certain period of time, seldom less than six months. In a country like Canada, with a large labour force in seasonal industries such as farming, logging, and construction, tens of thousands of men had no established residence and therefore came under no aid-giving jurisdiction. These became the transients of the early 1930s – 'Canada's Untouchables'[13] – riding the rails back and forth across the country, given the bum's rush from town to town, setting up in shacktowns outside city limits, panhandling and wandering. One class of the homeless could be dealt with handily: foreigners could be sent back where they came from. There were twenty-five thousand deportations between 1930 and 1934. The insistence on a policy of 'Canadians first' was one of the ugliest but most understandable reactions of the Canadian community to hardship. An undercurrent of bitter nativism foams up repeatedly in the Bennett letters.

In 1932 the federal government began to finance a system of work camps for single homeless men which soon came under the management of the Department of National Defence. Men worked eight hours a day in the camps building barracks, landing strips, roads, and other quasi-military projects in return for their board and lodging, clothing and medical service, plus an allowance of twenty cents a day. From 1933 to 1936 the population of the National Defence camps averaged about twenty thousand. Although one of the reasons for their establishment had been to stave off disorder and rioting by large numbers of homeless unemployed in the cities, the camps themselves became natural breeding-grounds for radical discontent. Twenty cents a day was closer to the wages of slave labour than to any minimum wage level in the country. Government protests that the money was never meant as wages and men could always leave the camps (and go hungry) fell on deaf ears. Military discipline was not being applied in the camps with a view to creating Canadian forces for the next war. But why then were the camps under the authority of the military? The camp system fell apart in 1935 when striking western relievers clashed with Mounted Police in Regina on Dominion Day in rioting that left one dead and fifty wounded. Mackenzie King's government ended the experiment in 1936. Despite their bad publicity then and since, the DND camps saved thousands of homeless from worse suffering. In 1939 the military would once more offer a haven of sorts for the residue of the decade's unemployed.[14]

Ever since Canadians had first begun to leave the farm for work in the cities, one reflexive response to hard times had been to go back to the land. The idea that somehow agriculture could take up the slack when industrial society broke down was one of the most prevalent, and by then one of the most anachronistic, notions of the 1930s. Beginning with the 'Colonization at Home Movement' of 1930 and the Relief Land Settlement Agreement of 1932, the Dominion government and every province except Prince Edward Island supported programs to establish would-be relievers on farm lands in Canada's unsettled regions. In theory the money spent to support a city family on relief in one year could make that family self-sustaining on a farm. Aside from one notable success with Dutch settlers on the marshland north of Toronto the back-to-the-land schemes were mostly tragic failures: again part of the tragedy echoes in some of the Bennett letters. A more successful complementary program placed unemployed men with farmers as hired help, but it worked only because the Dominion government paid each man's wages of $5 a month. When the farm placement system was expanded in 1936 after the camps closed down, the federal government found it had also to pay $5 a month to the farmers who took the men and then give every man who lasted the winter a $2.50 monthly bonus.[15] One of the hoariest and least accurate myths spread in Canadian history texts is that it was only backward-looking French-Canadian priests who called for a return to agriculture as a solution to the problems of modern society.

Literally hundreds of other programs were established to create work and alleviate suffering. These included debt-reduction legislation; loans to farmers, small businessmen, big businessmen, and homeowners; seed and fodder programs; job retraining schemes; subsidies to doctors and teachers to keep them on their jobs; the construction of the Trans-Canada Highway; and the war waged against drought and dust in Palliser's Triangle by the Prairie Farm Rehabilitation Administration after 1935. Aid programs became more sophisticated, precise, and effective as the depression wore on – partly because things were never again as bad as 1932-3, mostly because of the development of expertise and information that came from long years of groping with the problem of poverty (social work was everywhere a growth industry in the 1930s). By the standards of the modern welfare state all the programs were still very inadequate. This book shows beyond doubt that there were people not reached by any programs, and that there were Canadians in the depression who were both naked and starving. Still, the sickness of the 1930s was not quite unto death. Mortality rates kept on falling through the depression with the advance of medical science, and the $813 million spent by public authorities on relief between 1931 and 1937[16] did keep the bodies of the Canadian poor together. No one collected figures on the state of their souls.

4

By 1935 demands for fundamental reform in the Canadian economic system were coming from all sectors of the population – except a very few big-business leaders. Under the shifting, confused surface of reform agitation, most people had the same desires. Everyone's first thought in the 1930s was to protect his income. The major threat to a man's income was from competitors who offered to do the same job or sell the same product for less. Making that kind of competition impossible was the central legislative aim of organized labour, farmers, and small businessmen.

Minimum wage laws, for example, would guarantee that no one would be able to compete in the labour market by offering to work for less than a basic wage. Restrictions on working hours would have the same effect: no one could undercut a man by offering to work longer for the same pay. Similarly the farm movement all through North America had realized by the 1930s that the best strategy for maintaining income was 'orderly marketing.' This was a euphemism for farmers agreeing to stop competing with one another in the marketing of a crop and handle it through a central agency or 'marketing board.' To be effective the marketing board would have to have the force of law behind it to compel the price-cutting farmer to join the scheme, creating a producer's monopoly in the crop to be marketed.

In some ways the most interesting agitation to limit competition came from organizations of small businessmen who managed to attract the most national coverage of their plight and the least national comprehension. When Harry Stevens, Bennett's minister of trade and commerce, began his campaign against the buying practices of big business in 1934 – leading to the sensational revelations of his Royal Commission (at first a Select Committee) on Price Spreads he was acting as little more than a mouthpiece for organizations of retail merchants and small manufacturers. Ever since the rise of department and chain stores in the late 1880s small businessmen had been decrying the competitive methods of these organizations, claiming that their 'unfair' competition through the use of volume buying, loss leaders, and massive advertising deprived the legitimate retailer of his right to make a 'living' profit. For thirty years small business organizations had been lobbying for legislation restricting these competitive methods, as well as amendments to the anti-combine laws to permit their trade associations legally to fix prices.

This program was accepted by the Stevens Commission. Its recommendations to end 'predatory price-cutting' and legalize schemes of 'industrial self-government' (the business euphemism equivalent to 'orderly marketing') supervised by a Federal Trade and Industry Commission, would have severely limited competition in merchandising, crippling department and chain stores, and perhaps transferring monopoly powers to organizations of small business-men. Since wages and working conditions in small businesses were no better, probably worse, than in large companies (though the Stevens Commission carefully avoided comparisons), it is hard to see how the worker would have benefited from such a transfer of power. Nor would the consumer have profited from exchanging the cheap, efficient service of Eaton's and Simpson's for the expensive and inefficient business methods of the independent merchant. In general, it was not evident that the demands of any of the major interest groups, taken singly, would have been in the public interest or helped many of the people who appear in this book.

In the light of these campaigns, all directed at establishing controls to frustrate the workings of the free market, Bennett's 'New Deal' legislation of 1935 had neither the sudden virgin birth nor the radical overtones commentators then and since have assigned it. What Bennett gave the nation in 1935, along with his agricultural program of 1934, was a package deal of regulations and controls designed to give each major economic interest group the kind of government support it had long been demanding. By the Natural Products Marketing Act of 1934 farmers got the legal right to establish national marketing boards to close off the free market in agricultural produce. Workingmen had floors set against competition in wages and hours of work by the Minimum Wage Act, the Limitation of Hours of Work Act, and the Weekly Rest in Industrial Undertakings Act. The Dominion Trade and Industry Act — so often forgotten by students of Bennett's 'New Deal' — established the Trade and Industry Commission recommended by the Stevens Commission, and amendments to the Combines Investigation Act and the Criminal Code established the legal conditions small businessmen needed to counter-attack against the department and chain stores. The only major piece of legislation outside this framework was the Employment and Social Insurance Act establishing the national system of unemployment insurance that everyone knew was the only sensible way to rationalize the relief system (it would not, however, cover the currently unemployed).

Bennett's reform program was criticized by the right as socialism and by the left as 'state capitalism.' It was neither: it was an infusion of collectivism into Canadian economic life, partly consolidating existing restrictions on the free market, partly establishing new regulations and controls designed to aid major economic groups in their struggle against the forces of competition. As Bennett said repeatedly in his radio addresses that January of 1935, the enemy – the 'system' – was laissez-faire. He had not turned against capitalism *per se*. Instead he had adopted the deep anti-competitive traditions of the small capitalist – personified in Harry Stevens and his backers – at the same time as he was willing to give workers and farmers equal rights to conspire against the market place. The fact that these collectivist arrangements would have meant considerable restrictions on individual liberty gave rise to deep soul-searching amongst Parliamentarians on the meaning of liberalism and a liberal society. With Bennett's 'New Deal' Canada went further along the road to a collectivized economy than it ever had or has in peacetime. It was the same road Americans had set out on in 1933 when Roosevelt permitted the cartelization of his economy under the National Recovery Administration. The Germans and Italians came to one end of the same road under fascism.

None of these statutes would have brought export markets back to Canada or stimulated job-creating domestic expansion. From the day it was announced, most of the 'New Deal' appeared to be well beyond the constitutional powers of the federal government. Although there were the inevitable outcries against 'ignorant foreign judges,' no one was particularly surprised when the Judicial Committee of the British Privy Council struck down the bulk of Bennett's reforms in January 1937. The legislation that survived, mainly the limitations on free competition in business, was repealed by the Mackenzie King government to protect the public against conspiracy in restraint of trade. Careful examination of provincial statute books for the 1930s, however, would reveal dozens of items of 'mini-New Deal' legislation establishing labour standards, marketing boards, and price codes in industries ranging from pulp and paper manufacturing through fruit-growing and hair-dressing. In some measure, usually underestimated by historians, the provinces did respond to Canadians' search for ways to control the devastating forces of competition.

5

By 1935 R. B. Bennett had promised too much and delivered too little that was credible. The depression had exhausted his political capital with the voters. His own bullying, egotism, and inability to delegate authority had driven away many of his party and personal friends. It is not yet known whether the lonely bachelor toiling in his office or munching candy and reading Scripture in his suite at the Chateau Laurier ever understood what was happening to the country he governed. A letter he wrote in October 1931, explicitly reflecting the values of 1881, suggests he did not:

The difficulty about all these matters is that too much reliance is being placed upon the Government. The people are not bearing their share of the load. Half a century ago people would work their way out of their difficulties rather than look to a government to take care of them. The fibre of some of our people has grown softer and they are not willing to turn in and save themselves. They now complain because they have no money. When they were earning money many of them spent it in speculation and in luxury. 'Luxury' means anything a man has not an immediate need for, having regard to his financial position.

I do not know what the result of the present movement may be, but unless it induces men and women to think in terms of honest toil rather than in terms of bewilderment because of conditions which they helped to create, the end of organized society is not far distant.[17]

Perhaps Bennett had changed by 1935 and was wholeheartedly committed to the collectivism he was proposing to end the old order. Few Canadians believed that he was.

The only question mark surrounding Mackenzie King's return to power would be whether the three new parties contesting the election that October would deny him a majority government. Ominous as it appeared, the fragmentation of the Canadian political system by 1935 under depression pressures is easily exaggerated. The most successful 'third party' in terms of the popular vote, Harry Stevens' Reconstruction party (he had broken with Bennett, and his business allies were still disgruntled), elected only one member, Harry Stevens, and disappeared immediately. Social Credit was too ridiculous to be taken seriously outside of the prairies where the real world was too heartbreaking to take seriously. Only 9 per cent of the electorate agreed that the CCF spoke for the real interests of the masses: Canadian socialism, like the economy, was in bad shape for the rest of the depression and profited considerably from the transfiguration of war.

After 1935 the Mackenzie King government avoided the worst errors of the Bennett régime, closing the relief camps, stopping the deportations, ending the political oppression. It built slowly on the accumulating experience of the social workers, constitutional lawyers, and Keynesian economists. By 1938 the newly 'nationalized' Bank of Canada was gradually expanding the money supply and federal fiscal policy was beginning to be run on approved Keynesian contra-cyclical principles. The reciprocal trade agreements of 1935 and 1938 with the United States continued the slow rebuilding of Canada's trading relations. The Rowell-Sirois Commission was at work plotting to free the Dominion government from the shackles of an archaic constitution. The National Employment Commission had produced the first hard national statistics on problems of unemployment and relief and had underlined the desirability of direct federal action in the future. With the introduction of national unemployment insurance in 1940 and family allowances in 1945 the government of Canada was finally ready to fight the Great Depression.

6

Depending so heavily on written sources, historians have almost no first-hand access to the lives of the bottom groups in societies. Until the twentieth century few of the very poor were literate. Those who were had little to say, or, more properly, no one to hear them. People who tried to speak for the helpless – union leaders, social

workers, radical politicians – too often sketched the poor in their
own image. Even the oral history approach that relies on the
memories of those who suffered in the 1930s is vulnerable to the
distortions that a quarter-century of affluence has done to people's
remembrance of hard times (how often the comfortable remember
how adversity moulded character! those were great days!). These
letters to R. B. Bennett are unique in allowing us to bypass the
middle-class spokesmen for the under-people and enter directly into
their condition and feelings. These are the wretched of the 1930s
speaking for themselves. They speak more personally, more vividly,
more effectively than any source we know. We have changed their
names and often disguised their residence to protect their privacy.

The 168 letters reprinted here have been culled from several
thousand in the R. B. Bennett Papers in the Public Archives of
Canada. The selection was not made on a rigid statistical basis –
percentage quotas for each province, each category of poverty, each
year, and so on. That would have imposed an artificial straitjacket
on our desire to include the broadest and most interesting
cross-section of the correspondence. Since it appears that only a
fraction of the letters Bennett received from ordinary Canadians was
preserved in his papers, and there is no clue to the principles used in
that initial sorting, little of statistical value would have been gained
by doggedly quantifying an already unknown factor. But within the
limits of an impressionistic method we have preserved roughly the
same proportions of letters from regions, age and occupational
groups, people in need of jobs, money, clothes, etc., that are found
in the Bennett Papers. The bias in our selection does favour the
desperately poor. Many of Bennett's correspondents were 'normally'
underemployed, ill-fed, and ill-housed. To show the nether extremes
of Canadian life in the 1930s we deliberately give space to those who
suffered and needed the most. The letters are arranged in chronological order and in rough chronological proportion to the master
collection in Ottawa.

Bennett's three secretaries, sometimes the prime minister himself,
replied to almost every letter that had a return address. Most
answers, like that to Thomas Gibbs' first letter in the collection,
were suggestions to apply to municipal or provincial authorities. A
few others were regretful refusals of help. We have included every
reply that contains an unusual response to the writer's request or

adds details to our knowledge of Bennett's philanthropy and
personal feelings. We have also noted every instance in which money
was sent to a correspondent.

R. B. Bennett was already well off in 1921 when he inherited a
large holding in the E. B. Eddy paper companies from his long-time
friend, Jennie Shirreff Eddy. Her brother's shares came to him in
1926, totalling a several-million-dollar controlling interest in the
company. His income dropped sharply from its peak of $269,985 in
1929, but was never less than $150,000 annually in the 1930s.[18] His
philanthropies extended far beyond the $2 and $5 gifts recorded
here; one estimate sets his support of charitable organizations at
$25,000 annually.[19] One of Bennett's secretaries reported 'great
difficulty in restraining him from sending money to everyone who
asks for assistance.'[20] The necessary restraint seems to have been
exercised through the establishment of a special fund for these small
gifts, to be usually doled out by the secretaries without reference to
the prime minister. Other reports of Bennett's giving – that in-
scribed silver christening mugs were automatic rewards for naming a
child 'Richard Bedford,' that he was at one time supporting the
education of eighteen young people, and that his Christmas mailings
included twenty-five dozen boxes of candy, a hundred floral gifts,
and cheques totalling over $1,000[21] – round out a picture of
routinized but generous giving.

The volume of both letters and return donations increased as
Bennett's term wore on, reaching a sharp peak just before the
election of 14 October 1935 (in this case we presume that the
selection in the Bennett Papers accurately mirrors what happened).
Even though 1932 and 1933 were the worst years of the depression,
it is understandable that letters reflecting the limits of people's
endurance would increase after more years of bleak disappointment.
But it was also true that reports of Bennett's generosity had spread
by word of mouth and had appeared in the newspapers. This did
encourage letters to the prime minister. By 1935 a significant
proportion of the correspondents are nakedly begging for help.
Probably some of this was mail-order panhandling, but nothing has
impressed us more than the transparent authenticity of 95 per cent
of the letters we have read.

By election time, as well, some of Bennett's correspondents were
frankly offering to trade votes for aid (the whole collection testifies

to the honestly self-interested politics that poor people have to practise). Since the numbers of $5 responses also increased directly as election day neared – by October almost any plea with a return address seemed to touch the prime minister's secretaries – it is not unfair to reason that Bennett and his aides had also realized the vote-getting side-effects of philanthropy. The only other patterns we could find in the responses were a clear sympathy for the very young and slight tendencies to favour westerners before anyone, anglophones before francophones. In many cases there is no conceivable reason why one letter should receive a response and the plea of an equally desperate writer be filed away and forgotten.

What do these letters tell us about poverty in the Great Depression? They certainly indicate how bad the 1930s were for some people in Canada: worse, perhaps, than most of the history texts and even many of the survivors remember. To avoid exaggeration it must be emphasized that this is not a typical group of Canadians in the 1930s. The whole country was not in rags and starving. These are the forgotten people, the submerged tenth, and no description of Canadian life in the 1930s is balanced without including the other eight or nine million Canadians with whom we are not concerned. On the other hand written sources will never show what was happening to illiterate people in Canada during these years. There are no Indians or Eskimoes represented in this portrait of the wretched of Canada who could read and write.

A few generalizations can be drawn from this admittedly impressionistic sample. Some recurring themes in the letters have already been mentioned: overtones of resentment at foreigners, children being kept out of school for lack of clothing, the inadequacy of relief, the back-biting and stinginess of the petty. Veterans of the Great War tend to wonder what they fought for; there are isolated instances of generosity and humanity; the young seem always hopeful. The over-representation of rural areas in the collection suggests that urban relief was more effective in alleviating suffering. The letters also show the obvious but usually forgotten phenomenon of the worst burdens falling on the shoulders of those least able to bear them. Age, sickness, and fecundity were handicaps to economic survival in the best of times. In the depression they were the hallmarks of hopelessness. The old age pension in the 1930s was $20 a month to the needy over seventy; there was no such thing as medical insurance; contraception was a dirty word, particularly in Quebec. The one ironic consolation of having a large family in the 1930s was that the relief given a man with six, eight, or ten children was sometimes more than he could earn at a full-time job.

Bennett's correspondents tend to be humble, proud, and God-fearing folk. Some spirits have been broken, but only a handful are striking out in rage and despair. Perhaps most of the letters received (or kept) by a Conservative prime minister would be from conservative, deferential people. But perhaps the Canadian people as a whole had too much discipline, too much individualism, too much nineteenth-century grit, or too little political sophistication to fight back in radical protest against a whole economic and social system. Maybe this was what the CCF never understood about the Canadian people.

Finally, these letters strip away the tawdry glamour and stupid nostalgia that somehow clouds the 1930s in retrospect. The lives of these people are bleak and still. There is little mobility in this book, barely more than the dirt-cheap tourism of the boxcar. Even the ordinary escape-hatches of the radio, the newspaper, the cinema, and liquor have been closed for many of them. They can't even afford a fantasy world. Theirs is life at the bottom, a single-minded struggle for survival, monotonous and dreary. The depression is suffocating. They write to Ottawa late at night, and hope.

L. M. Grayson
Michael Bliss
May 1971

NOTES

1 National Employment Commission, *Final Report* (Ottawa, 1938), pp. 105-10; James H. Gray, *The Winter Years* (Toronto, 1966), p. 35.
2 M. C. Urquhart, ed., *Historical Statistics of Canada* (Toronto, 1965), p. 178.
3 *Ibid.*, p. 357.
4 Lothar Richter, ed., *Canada's Unemployment Problem* (Toronto, 1939), p. 9. If the whole labour force is counted, the figure is 826,000 or 19.3 per cent — Urquhart, *Historical Statistics*, p. 61.

5   Leonard C. Marsh, *Canadians In and Out of Work* (Montreal, 1940), p. 296.
6   Harry M. Cassidy, *Social Security and Reconstruction in Canada* (Toronto, 1943), p. 40; Richter, *Canada's Unemployment Problem*, p. 34.
7   National Employment Commission, *Final Report*, p. 110.
8   University of Toronto Archives, H. M. Cassidy Papers, Box 24, Cassidy to D. R. Michener, 25 March 1933.
9   Richter, *Canada's Unemployment Problem*, pp. 78-84.
10   H. M. Cassidy, *Unemployment and Relief in Ontario, 1929-32* (Toronto, 1932), p. 175; Gray, *The Winter Years*, passim; A. Lawton, 'Relief Administration in Saskatoon during the Depression,' *Saskatchewan History*, XXII, 1969, p. 44; Blair Neatby, 'The Saskatchewan Relief Commission, 1931-34,' in D. Swainson, ed., *Historical Essays on the Prairie Provinces* (Toronto, 1971), p. 275.
11   Cassidy, *Unemployment and Relief in Ontario*, p. 185; Richter, *Canada's Unemployment Problem*, p. 102-3.
12   Gray, *The Winter Years*, passim.
13   The title of a pamphlet by Rev. Andrew Roddan, published in Vancouver in 1932.
14   Richter, *Canada's Unemployment Problem*, pp. 181-5; James Eayrs, *In Defence of Canada: From the Great War to the Great Depression* (Toronto, 1964), pp. 124-48.
15   Richter, *Canada's Unemployment Problem*, pp. 185-6, 261-95.
16   Urquhart, *Historical Statistics*, p. 37.
17   Public Archives of Canada, R. B. Bennett Papers, 490588, Bennett to J. G. Bennett (no relation), 21 Oct. 1931.
18   Ernest Watkins, *R. B. Bennett* (Toronto, 1963), p. 93.
19   *Ibid.*, p. 245.
20   Andrew D. Maclean, *R. B. Bennett* (Toronto, 1935), p. 26.
21   Watkins, *R. B. Bennett*, p. 244; Maclean, *R. B. Bennett*, p. 27.

ACKNOWLEDGMENTS

We are grateful to the Harriet Irving Library, University of New Brunswick, Fredericton, for permission to use the letters from R. B. Bennett which are part of the Bennett Papers. The Bennett Papers are now temporarily housed in the Public Archives of Canada for indexing, and we acknowledge with thanks the co-operation of both institutions in allowing us access to the letters and assisting us in working with them.

The letters from the people of Canada to Mr Bennett are, in law, in the copyright of those who wrote them. It would have been a forlorn and despairing task to seek them or their descendants in order to obtain permission to reproduce the letters, but we now record our gratitude to them for their writings and acknowledge our indebtedness. We apologize for not attempting the impossible, but we have tried to protect privacy by altering the names of people and places whenever it seemed necessary to do so; these fictional names do, however, seek to maintain the character, ethnic or geographical, of the originals. The spelling and punctuation of the original letters have been followed as closely as possible. The numbers after each letter in the text are the page numbers of the original in the Bennett Papers.

We also thank Mr John Weiler who, as our research assistant, made the initial selection from the Bennett Papers.

LG and MB

The wretched of Canada

Sarnia Ont.
Dec 1st/30

Hon. Mr. Bennet
Ottawa Ont.

Dear Sir:
I am taking this priviledge in my own hands of writing you which a
person of my class should be ashamed to take such athoraty. But I
am down and out and do not know what to do. We have six children
and I don't beleive it right to see them suffer for the want of food I
tried everywhere to get things for them to eat this is Saturday and I
must say we have to go all day Sunday with but one small meal that
is dry bread and apple sauce which we have day after day the apples
will soon run out then we will be out of luck. I asked for asistance
from the township they never came near me. I was in the second
Canadian infantry Battalion as a private. I wrote to London see if
I could get releif there. Enclosed you will find a coppy which they
sent me. I will not take up too much of your time just now. But in
my case I am a good worker but the work is not to be had. My
name has been in the employment office since June but there is no
jobs comming in so I have to do something might soon I hate to go
out and steal but the family can't starve to death. I am a butcher by
trade and know cattle, and understand them thourghly. Also farmed
for twelve years. Am willing to go anywhere to work if there is
anything at all you can possible do for me this will be greatly appreciated if there is any dought these statements call Sarnia 1154 that
will be Mr. A.E.Palmer Employment Bureau. Kindly over look the
privledge Im taking I think this is my last chance to get help. If this
fails I do not know what we will do.
    Thanking you very kindly in advance.

Yours very Truly,
Thomas M. Gibbs

395690-2

[Reply]

Ottawa, December 11th, 1930

Dear Sir,
I beg to acknowledge receipt of your letter of December 1st
addressed to the Prime Minister, who has not yet returned from
attending the Imperial Conference and, therefore, cannot reply to
you himself.

I have made inquiries regarding your case and find that the
answer given to you by the Assistant District Administrator of the
Westminster Hospital, in London, Ontario, was quite correct, and
that no relief is given by the Department except to pensioners.

As you know, money was voted by Parliament at the special
session for the purpose of providing unemployment relief. This is
arranged, in the first instance, through the municipality, which takes
it up with the Province, and then it is placed before the Dominion
Government.

I suggest that you give the details of your case to the municipal
authorities in Sarnia, and ask them to assist you in your difficulties.

Yours faithfully,
Private Secretary

Thomas M. Gibbs, Esquire,
Sarnia, Ontario

395696

Sherbrooke
Pro. Que
Canada
Jan. 5th. 1931

Rt. Hon. R.B.Bennett.
Prime Minister of Canada

Dear Sir:
Always beining Conservetive and hearing you speak in the 54th
Armory Belveredere St. Sharbrooke when you were here; I am
taking this time to write you: I am a painter and paper hanger and
Decorator by trade: I havent done any work since June 28th 1930;
I have a Wife and three girls ages 13 yrs 11 yrs and 9 yrs. My Wifes
family in Lincolnshire England have been helping us out; Ive been
going and regoing to the City to get work: all I get is We will see
what can be done: Our rent is back from Nov. Dec. 1930 and this
month God only knows where are going to get it from: I have asked
& asked the City to help, and they say its been turned down for
some reason the reason they wont tell: Today I whent to get 3$ to
keep us for a week and Mr Valcourt of the City Office said I couldn't
get it because someone said we had a radio: We have never had a
radio: He sent Mr. Lesseau from the City Office to search our home
from top to bottom bedrooms and bathroom under and over: Then
he says he don't have to give us help if he dont want to: I ask you
Sir "who was this money given to and what for"? is it for a man to
crawl on his hands and knees to get a loaf for his family:? I ask you
Sir how do you think we live on $3 a week and can't get that
because some people make up a lie: What sort of a country have we:
I dont want help: I want work I'll do anything to keep my family.
A few lines from you would be a good help Thanking you for your
time

I beg
To Remain.
A disheartened Man
P.W.L. Norton

393898-9

Calgary Alta
April 7th 1931

The Honorable R.B.Bennet
Premier
Ottawa

Honorable Sir:
As I understand you believe in fair Play I would like to know how
the Civic Relief Dept. expects a person to manage to clothe & feed
a family of seven children on the stipend they give. The food part
was sufficient after Dr Roach informed them the physical condition
the children were in from Malnuttrition. We have received the sum
of $8 per week for groceries two for milk & two for meat. The latter
very recently as all thru February we received no meat allowance at
all. That part was alright also $20.00 per month rent.

But how are we to cloth them. As we buy our own food while
working for money. Buy street car tickets for both Civil Relief &
Cash relief.

The eldest child a boy of eleven is suffering from indigestion &
nerves for which we have had to have prescription filled by Dr
Acton's Orders. The baby a girl of 2½ is considerable underweight
as she only weighs 21 lbs. I have always done my best to give them
the necessary food nor have they ever had any luxuries as my
occupation has always been seasonal & we have had to deny them
most of the necessities all summer to catch up back debts of Light,
Water rent & sometimes groceries.

We have always had an investigator here each time we have made
application for Civic Relief. However I know of one person at least
who receives his Cash Relief. His Civic relief food & partial rent &
his wife works steady getting a salary of $49.00 per month & they
have just three children. Naturally they have luxuries such as tinned
lobster, apples oranges etc.

I have worked out my direct relief & have been glad to do so,
however what I need is a regular job I am a good mechanic & have
usually serviced for machine companies in the five years I have been
here But have always been willing to do any kind of work at all. I
was born in Stormont Co Ont & my father also & my wifes' parents
& her grandparents were born there too. We have always been

supportors of the Conservative Party & it seems pretty tough if we can't get a job, a steady one while we see Americans come over & fill jobs that Canadians should have.

A Mr Ruggles was brought over by the Manager of the Olivier Co last Spring & has held a steady job ever since Altho he is supposed to be a super-service man he is about the poorest on the staff But his services were retained last winter while all other service men were laid of. While there is just him & his wife while I have eight dependents of British descent. Not only that but when a Canadian would make an application for a job he was told in at least one instance He wasn't hiring any one just then but if he did he wanted men from Kansas.

I realize you are a very busy & important man & I am taking up valuable time but I feel that for my childrens sake at least I must let you know underr what conditions we have carried on. If you know of any opening where I would be likely to get work I would be very happy.

Your humble servant
Ralph A. Mackenzie

The Civil Relief refused us food tickets as they consider we got too much in March. Are the children to starve. I have the merchants word I never bought luxuries.

71772-5

Inverness, Ont. R2
April 22nd, 31

Hon R.B.Bennett
Ottawa, Can.

Honorable & Dear Sir/
I hope this letter of mine may reach you, instead of being dropped into the Waste Paper Basket.

I saw last week in a paper that you had given to your sister, Miss
Mildred, a wedding gift of $2,000,000. How grand it must have been
to be able to do that! I thought what a lot of money you must have,
and I wondered if you would lend to me and my brother some
money — say $10,000.

My brother owns a farm, but it was mortgaged when he got it,
and he has not been able to lift the mortgage.

He owns between 50 & 60 head of Shorthorn cattle, most of
them pure-bred, of all ages. He has also more than 20 head of horses
— good Clydes, pure-bred. One would ask why not sell some of
this stock, but people here have not the money to buy.

I am a school teacher, but had to give up my work, on account
of ill health, so I can not help Everett. I am writing this letter as I
lie in bed.

$10,000 seems an awful amount to ask to borrow all at once,
but it would let us free of debt except to you, and perhaps you
could wait until we could get it for you, when times improve —

I am, yours truly
Muriel Telman

[Reply]

Ottawa, 25th April 1931

Dear Miss Telman:

I assure you there is no truth in the rumor to which you have
directed attention in your letter of the 22nd April, and I have been
caused a great deal of distress by reason of the publication of that
story.

I regret that I am not in a position to be of the service to you
which you suggest. I have received a very great number of such
appeals.

I am sorry to hear of your illness, and I trust that before long you
will have completely regained your health.

With best wishes to your brother and yourself, I am

Yours faithfully,
R.B.Bennett

396949-51

Ottawa, May 7, 1931

Dear Mr. Bennett, —

I am going to ask you to do me a great favour. I am one of the
Temporary Stenographers who were laid off because of your order
to reduce the staffs.

I was in the Department of Public Works, Secretary's Branch,
from June 21st, 1930, to March 20, 1931. Since then I have not
been able to secure work anywhere, although I have tried very hard.
They all seem to be over-staffed.

I am a widow with three children to support, and as they are very
young and all going to school it strikes me very hard. The eldest is
11 years and the youngest 7 years.

I am up against it now, the merchants have closed my accounts
because I was unable to pay them last month, that means I will
starve as I charged my groceries.

Perhaps I should mention the fact that my father is a staunch
Conservative and has been one all his life. If you wish to know just
how hard my father has worked for the Conservative Party ask Mr.
McGillis, M.P. for Glengarry. I am from St. Anne, Ont., but have
lived here for the past twelve years. My father's name is Charles
Gaspard.

Will you please help me to get a position in the Civil Service for
it is a case of getting work at once or starving. I know that you are
the only one that can help me now.

I am enclosing copy of a letter that I wrote Mr. McGillis before I
was laid off.

Trusting that you will help me,

I remain,
Yours sincerely,
Anne McAndrew

394364-5

Southwark, Alta.,
May 16th, 1931

Honourable R.B.Bennett, Esq.,
Ottawa, Canada.

Honourable Sir;
    I am enclosing herewith, a letter received by this Council on May 13th., asking for relief from this Village.
    The Village have given this man what relief they could through the winter and at the present time, they are absolutely unable to continue further relief.
    The Councillors have looked into this matter and have found conditions in his house to be as stated in the enclosed letter. There is no doubt that this man is in desperate need of immediate relief and he is willing to do any work to feed and cloth his wife and family, but there is no work at the present time.

We are respectfully petitioning you to give this matter your immediate attention,

Yours respectfully,
H.W.Manfred   Reeve
J. Johnson   Councillor
W.H. Hazeltine   Councillor

[Enclosure]

Southwark, Alberta, May 13th 1931

TO THE REEVE AND COUNCILLORS OF THE VILLAGE OF
SOUTHWARK ALBERTA CANADA.

Gentlemen:
I wish to bring to your immediate notice the present condition of my family. I am a married man, with three children aged 8, 5 and 5 respectively, dependant upon me. I am a BONA FIDE returned soldier, having served in the Canadian Expeditionary Forces as a VOLUNTEER, and not as a conscript, in the front line trenches in 1915, and was finally discharged in April 1919 as medically unfit. I do not receive an army pension. I hold the Mons Medal, The Canadian General Service and The Victory Medals of the last war, also the Class "A" France-button and the Class "B" (England) button. I have proper documentary evidence of ALL the foregoing statements available for your verification if necessary. At present there is in my house the following NECESSITIES, (and NO LUXURIES)

Bread	2 home-made loaves	Flour	NONE
Yeast	NONE	Dried raisins	½ a packet
Sugar	NONE for past 3 days	Butter	NONE
Fat, Dripping, Lard, etc.	NONE	Meat	None, have had 40¢
Vegetables,	About half bag, potatoes,	worth in past six	
	None of any other kind.	weeks.	
Tea	2 ounces	Coffee, cocoa, etc,	NONE
Soap	NONE OF ANY KIND, Neither toilet nor laundrey.		
Milk	About 2 quarts	Oatmeal	about 3 lbs

Salt   5 cents worth   Wheat   about 3 lbs.
Syrup, Honey, Jam, Peanut butter
or other "Spreads for bread"   NONE
Eggs   ONE DOZEN.   Note: On Sunday evening May 3rd we had
164 eggs showing that we have eaten 152 eggs in past 9 days or over
3 eggs each per day. Yesterday noon my wife and children arrived
at the point where they could no longer eat the eggs and keep them
down. It is more than a week since any of my family had butter on
their bread, the previous week they had one pound, kindly GIVEN
by a local friend.

As you are aware, I have received "relief" from the village during
the past winter amounting to about 39 dollars, of which I have
"Worked-off" about 24 dollars, the remainder of which I am willing
and anxious to work off at any time, or to repay when I am able. I
would have applied to you for further relief, had I not received your
recent letter stating your inability to issue any more relief. I am
informed that demands or requests upon the Federal Government
for relief must be passed up through the proper channels, in this
case the village in which I reside.

I am forwarding a copy of this letter to Ottawa, and am
requesting that you, the REEVE and both councillors will visit my
house in person, and at once, to check over the food in my possession, and verify the foregoing statements, and then immediately
communicate with the Federal Relief Board on our behalf. Tomorrow I am withdrawing my 8 year old son from school attend-
ance, as he is not getting enough nourishment to permit of his being
able to study, and furthermore we have no soap to wash him or
ourselves, or any of our clothes.

Thanking you for your kind assistance in the past, and assuring
you that I would prefer remunerative work to charity, I am,

Gentlemen,
Very truly yours,
Richard J. O'Hearn

No. 94317
Late member of the
following CANADIAN ARMY UNITS.

45th Victoria Reg. Ontario
25th Battn. Ontario.
11th Overseas Battalion of Montreal, England,
    France and Belgium
16th Bn. C.G.R. Calgary, and the
CANADIAN MILITARY POLICE CORPS.

I might add that when the Honourable R.B.Bennett spoke over the
radio here in the West recently I heard him state that "No man who
served his country in the war should want for food shelter or fuel."
I would further add that I have not spent 2 dollars on beer in over
2 years, I and my family have not attended a single dance, show, or
ball game during the past winter except one concert where we took
part in the performance. The residents of this village can verify this.

490384-6

May 20/31

Mr Bennette
    Since you have been elected, work has been imposible to get.
We have decided that in a month from this date, if thing's are the
same, We'll skin you alive, the first chance we get

Sudbury Starving Unemployed

484936

Pembroke, Ont.
July 12, 1931.

Dear Premier Bennett;–

I am a young man at the age of twenty-four and a strong Conservative. I neither drink or indulge in the habbit of smoking. The only condition is that my sight isn't perfected but that shouldn't be any reason why to prevent me from making good in this world if I had a chance to.

I wonder if you could possible manage to secure me a position in some office or factory down there in Ottawa among the business men without causing any inconvenience to yourself or outside feelings toward me.

For since I had the operation on my eyes last Oct. the farm work is far to strenuous and havy for me to do. It strains my eyes to much.

I would be so thankful if you could obtain me a job of some description for I have tried all over myself. I would a thousand times work for my living then to draw a pention. Please excuse my boldness for taking the privilege of writting direct to you. I am so anxious to have a chance to do something for myself. So if you hear tell of anything within the next two weeks will you kindly let me know?

Yours very truly and obliging,
Roger Johnston

[Reply]

Ottawa, July 14th, 1931.

Dear Mr. Johnston,

I have before me your letter of the 12th of July and greatly regret to hear that your eyes are giving you trouble. This seems a pity for I would imagine farm work, at the present time, offers more inducements than work in the city.

The truth is, however, at the moment I know of no vacancy to which I could direct your attention and, if I know of any, I would

be only too glad to let you know. But conditions at the present time
are such that it is difficult to obtain a position even though many
applicants have the necessary qualifications and training.

I trust your eyesight will greatly improve, and with best wishes,
believe me, I am,

Yours faithfully,
R.B.Bennett

395051-3

Kent Ont.
December 15, 1931

Hon. R.B.Bennett
Royal York, Toronto

Dear Mr. Bennett,—I hope you will pardon my writing to you today.

I saw in the Toronto Star where you were going to be the speaker
on Wednesday night at the Royal York so have taken the liberty to
write to you and I hope you will regard this as strictly confidential.

I am glad you arrived home safely from your trip abroad and hope
it has done you good.

Would like to hear your talk but have no radio.

You will wonder what in the world I have written to you about.

Well, we are farmers. We came out to this place about five years
ago to try our hand at farming.

My man has a trade at carpentering but he developed rheumatism
in the shoulders, caused I believe by the constant use of hammer
and saw, so we thought a change of work, using other muscles might
be good for him.

We traded our home, equity 2300. on this farm but found after
moving here that the place had been terribly neglected and was in a
very run down condition. We have worked very hard and it shows a
marked improvement but we seem unable to get far ahead.

There are several buildings which could be renovated but the

folks who hold the mortgages will not let us tear them away to
improve the rest and we feel it is not fair for us to put on improve-
ments, not having the privilege of using what could be used here as
well.

Last year I sent $12. to the Agricultural Development Board
asking for a loan but they replied they were sorry they could not
let us have it but *hoped* we could get it somewhere else. Now, Mr.
Bennett, I ask you, what is the use of trying to get on if the Government refuses help to their own Canadian born sons and daughters. I
suppose if we were Doukobours, Emigrants or most anything else,
we would be set up and given a chance. We have done all we can to
be decent, honorable, and to raise our family to be a credit to the
country, but what's the use. On every hand we get a knock. What I
want to do is get a start with chickens. We had a lovely flock when
on No 7 Highway but after Mother died I had to go home for a while
and one Sunday night—while my husband came to see us, some
person came and took everything. We have lost heart but I am
beginning again to get a flock together. There is a wonderful range
here for hens and geese but I think we will be having a foreclosure
soon and so hardly know what to do. The boys, our boys are twins
13 years old, want us to stay on the farm, but I am afraid we will
have no choice in the matter. Today, if it were to save my life, I
could not find one cent in the place. We own a note at the Bank for
$150. and one would imagine from the fuss that is made over it, that
it was $150.000.

The worry of all these things is driving me mad. God alone knows
how hard we have tried to get on but prices are no good now. If we
could borrow about $10.000 at 3% and pay off what we owe to
everybody we would still have plenty to fix up our farm and get a
start in chickens and a few good cows. We have all our implements
paid for and have 3 cows, 1 hiefer, 3 horses and a colt 1½ yrs old,
and all we owe on them is $50 altogether. We have had to sell our
two other young cows and two good sows to pay up but thank good-
ness we are that much farther out of debt.

Ours is I suppose only one case in hundreds but nevertheless it
doesn't alter our worries any. Is there nothing that can be done to
help out such cases. The unemployment situation is as bad on the
farms as anywhere but we never receive help in any way. Christmas
is only 10 days away and I haven't the first thing for any of the

youngsters and have nothing to get anything with. Many times I have been tempted to throw everything to the winds but something still seems to whisper "Keep on". What a wonderful thing Faith in God is. There is a little verse which seems to mean so much to me.

Courage, brother, do not stumble
Tho the path be dark as night
There's a star to guide the humble
Trust in God, and do the right.

Tho the road be dark and dreary
And the ending out of sight.
Step out boldly, glad or weary,
Trust in God, and do the right.

Isn't it beautiful? Please God I may always remember and do just that. Trust in God, and do the right.

Please Mr. Bennett, forgive me for sending this letter but somehow it eases my mind to send it.

I hope you have a very Merry Christmas.

Respectfully yours,
Dorothy Franklin

[Reply]

Ottawa, December 29, 1931

Dear Mrs. Franklin:

I cannot tell you how greatly I was concerned after reading your very excellent letter. It was the letter of a woman who had endured much, but had still maintained her courage and faith.

I have ventured to write the Minister of Agriculture at Toronto to see if something cannot be done to assist your family.

I regret the delay in answering you, but the truth is I dictated a reply the day your letter was received, but the notes were mislaid and it is only this morning that I was advised of that fact.

I trust the New Year may bring you great happiness and be an

entire change to the one you have just passed. With all good wishes
and kindest regards, I am,

Yours faithfully,
R.B.Bennett

[See also the letter from Mrs Franklin on p. 118.]

394444-9

Nanaimo B.C.
Feb 22nd

Mr Bennett

x x

Dear Sir
before we are much older there is going to be trouble in Nanaimo &
Cumberland owing to the foreigners having jobs while the men &
boys who are borne British subjects & who rightfully belong to these
jobs have to go without jobs therefore they have to go without
sufficient food & clothing, in Cumberland you have Japanese &
Chinese working in & about the mines also other foreigners from
other countrys who can neither read write or speak english & this
is breaking the Coal Mines Rules & Regulation Act & they are a
danger to both human life & property yet they hold the jobs which
rightfully belong to us British although it is against the rules for
these people to have jobs in the mines.
     The same applied to Nanaimo only the Chinese are working on
the surface here & not below but there are a very large number of
foreigners working in the mines at Nanaimo who can neither read
write nor speak English & apart from that besides having our jobs &
getting the wages which is ours by right the money is not only going
out of Nanaimo but it is going out of the country & that is not good
for this country. I wish you could come yourself to the mines at
Nanaimo & watch the ammount of foreigners who are employed at

these mines & then look at the number of British men & boys who
go to these same mines every day begging for a job only to be turned
away & they have no money to buy bread & clothing while the
foreigner has both the foreigners are also starting allkinds of stores &
boarding houses & trying to buy beer parlours while the Britisher
goes broke as there are not enough British men & boys in employment & the foreigner buys all from his own kind. It looks to me as
though the chief Superintendent of these mines here is trying to
cause a lot of trouble on this Island by employing as many foreigners
as possible at the expense of the people who belong to this country if
this is so he is going to see all the trouble & more than he wants
before long as human nature can't stand for it much longer there is a
lot of talk here (& men say they are prepared to prove it) that
Robert Fox who is superintendent of these mines is accepting bribes
from these foreigners for jobs. I hope goverment will take a hand in
this before it is too late as there is so much money going out of this
town & out of the country & our men & boys are asked to go to
goverment camps & give up their homes to these foreigners the
foreigner can come here & make a home while the men & boys who
have a right to a home & a job have to get out to make room for the
foreigner can you wonder that the Britisher is getting riled & again
very many of these foreigners fought against our men & boys in the
big war now they are given our jobs our bread & our homes if
goverment does not take a hand in this at once I fear an uprising of
all English speaking people on this Island & it may end in harm to
the foreigner & also to property

Yours. A.Nanaimoite

492119-20

Lantham Alberta
Feb 22, 1932.

Hon. R.B.Bennett
Ottawa, Ont.

My dear sir.
    Realizing as we all do these times, and willing as we are to do our
best, their is a limit to all things.
    In November 1930 I applied for work in Calgary, early in 1931 I
wrote to Parliament at Edmonton. (Public Works). I wrote both the
department of Education and the A.T.A. to secure a school. Last fall
I visited the Chief Engineer for these parts to see about work. I have
been a public school teacher in Alberta for nearly ten years, but
unfortunately tried for another school and lost. Just think of it. *"I
haven't had one days work since October 1930.* I have to support a
wife and three children." Pretty hard proposition for an honest
Canadian. Don't you think so? I am a born Canadian of the fourth
generation. I certainly would like a chance to make an honest living
at least.

Sincerely,
Ronald A. Stanton

396508

Ottawa
Marth the 4th 1932

Dear Sir,
    I am just writing a few lines to you to see what can be done for us
young men of Canada. We are the growing generation of Canada, but
with no hopes of a future. Please tell me why is it a single man
always gets a refusal when he looks for a job. A married man gets
work, & if he does not get work, he gets relief. Yesterday I got a

glimpse of a lot of the unemployed. It just made me feel down-
hearted. to think there is no work for them, or in the future, &
also no work for myself. Last year I was out of work three months. I
received work with a local farm. I was told in the fall I could have
the job for the winter; I was then a stable man. Now I am slacked off
on account of no snow this winter. Now I am wandering the streets
like a beggar, with no future ahead. There are lots of single men in
Ottawa, who would rather walk the streets, & starve, than work on a
farm. That is a true statement. Myself I work wherever I can get
work, & get a good name wherever I go. There are plenty of young
men like myself, who are in the same plight. I say again whats to be
done for us single men? do we have to starve? or do we have to go
round with our faces full of shame, to beg at the doors of the well to
do citizen. I suppose you will say the married men come first; I
certainly agree with you there. But have you a word or two to cheer
us single men up a bit? The married man got word he was going to
get relief. That took the weight of worry off his mind quite a bit.
Did the single man here anything, how he was going to pull through?
Did you ever feel the pangs of hunger? My Idea is we shall all starve.
I suppose you will say I cant help it, or I cant make things better.
You have the power to make things better or worse. When you
entered as Premier you promised a lot of things, you was going to do
for the country. I am waiting patiently to see the results. Will look
for my answer in the paper.

Yours Truly R.D. Ottawa

485899-900

The Honourable R.B.Bennet
Ottawa

March 15 1932
Banner Sask

Honourable Sir
   I take the liberty of addressing myself directly to you on a matter
of great importance to me. I have been trying to find out if there is
any government grant or private bounty on the occasion of the birth
of triplets. I am getting a little relief now but am very hard up and
the other week my wife gave birth to triplets & I would surely appr-
ciate it if you could inform me if there is any special fund for helping
on such an occasion. I have been told there is some such bounty or
grant, but can find out nothing definite, so I decided to find out
from head-quarters — I shall therefore greatly value any information
you may send me on this matter. I had four small children before
and now with the additional three I find it very hard to get along
and with conditions as they are I sure need some extra help.

I am
Yours respectfully
John A. Eldon

397883-4

General Delivery,
Winnipeg, Ma.
April 19th 1932

R.B.Bennett.
Ottawa, Ont.

Dear Sir:—
   I have written previous letters* to you personally and am awaiting
a reply.

I have been unemployed for 26 months and am married and have three children *all sick* ages 4 years, 2½ years, and 14 months.

We have lost our home, furniture and all during the 26 months of unemployment.

I was employed by the Manitoba Telephone System for some years since leaving school in 1914.

I was discharged on Feb. 25th 1930 and have not done any work since that time. On the 20th of February the city of Winnipeg refused to give me further assistance and since that time I have taken the matter up with Mr. J.D.MacGregor, W.R.Chubb, Mr. MacNamara all of the provincial Government.

I have followed Electrical Work throughout my life working in the various branches and have learned to drive many types of cars I have also worked upon the Great Lakes and have attained a Certificate of Able Seaman for Service upon Any Waters.

I was born in Winnipeg in 1901 of parents also born in Canada and am of British decent.

As I have mentioned the City of Winnipeg have refused to assist me further and the result is that we have had many a hungry day since then and now the landlord has placed us upon the Street and that is where I am now with my family.

I have a few devices which I have plans drawn for which if I were able to finance I could become independent and also any one whom cared to enter into it with me.

I have a number of them which I would like you to hear of and determine if such articles are of use or not to your own discretion.

One of them is to use upon an Automobile to notify a driver when he has only one headlight or to notify him of his tail light failing to burn.

Another one is a signal to place upon the car back and front to give the direction in which the car is going to turn and also notify the driver that that signal is being given it cannot remain in use after the turn is completed.

And others worthy of any persons investment on an equal basis— The second mentioned device is one that is required to prevent approximately 90 percent of all accidents caused by false signals.

Won't you please investigate my case and see that something is done at once?

Otherwise can you secure a position for me anywhere in Canada doing anything or consider my devices and place me in touch with someone whom will finance them.

Whatever you may do will truly be appreciated by my family and myself.

We are hungry, tired and desperate and cannot hold out any longer. Please it means so much to our children. We have no home and therefore cannot give any other address,

I am, Yours Truly,
Charles Grierson

[*They have not been found in the Bennett Papers.]

[Reply]

Ottawa, April 22, 1932

Charles Grierson, Esq.,
c/o General Delivery,
Winnipeg, Manitoba.

Dear Sir:

The Prime Minister has asked me to acknowledge the receipt of your letter of the 19th instant.

Mr. Bennett is very sorry to learn of the difficult circumstances through which you are passing at present and regrets that he does not know of anybody who would be interested in the development of your inventions. As far as employment is concerned, Mr. Bennett can only suggest that you keep in touch with the Winnipeg municipal authorities, as any arrangements for relief will be made through the provincial government who, in turn, deals direct with the municipality.

Yours faithfully,
Private Secretary

[See also letters from Grierson on pp. 46, 68, 151, 156, 161, 172.]

396043-9

Player, Sask.,
May 18th 1932

Hon. R.B.Bennet,
Ottawa, Ont.

Dear Sir,—
    I would be real pleased to be wearing a ball suit if you sent me
one. My sizes are as follows, Chest 34, Waste 32, size 7 shoes and a
cap size 22 inches. I am 5ft. 8 in and am 14 years old. The colors I
would like it are Black trimed with white and a P on the front. I am
hopping to receive it by the third of June because we are going to
play at a picnic. Thanking you in advance.

Yours truly,
Sean Kelly

[Reply]

Ottawa, June 13, 1932

Dear Sean:
    Your letter of the 18th May, addressed to the Prime Minister, is
before me for acknowledgment.
    I think you can understand how desperately rushed Mr. Bennett
is and how impossible it would be for him to get for you the
baseball suit you are anxious to have. I nevertheless enclose herewith
a five dollar bill with which I trust it may be possible for you to get
at least a part of this equipment.
    I hope you have a very nice summer and that when the Fall
comes you will give your best possible attention to your studies.
You appear to be a good sized young fellow for your years.
    With best wishes, I am

Yours faithfully,
Secretary.

399053-4

Easterton,
Ont.
May 29, 1932

Hon. R.B.Bennett
House of Commons
Ottawa
Canada

Dear Mr. Bennett,—
   I tried to see you several times while the House was in Session;
but I was unsuccessful: Mr. Bennett I need some help, and I feel that
you are the only one who can help me: I need some money to help
my Father:* He like others has suffered through this depression: and
unfortunately borrowed money from the Bank. and he has lost so
much money in this last three years that he can hardly keep up the
interest: It worries me so Mr. Bennett: as I feel the worry is too
great for him to bear: and I am afraid of him committing suicide and
I just could not let anything like that happen to him. Oh, Mr.
Bennett it is so hard in Public Life to owe money. it just leaves one
so handicapped: for there is so much expense in connection with
Public Life. I know you are sympathic, Mr. Bennett and a real good
Christian and you can do so much to help my Father and you could
make me the happiest girl in the world. Mr. Bennett I always ask
God to Bless you, and give you the very best Health and strength to
carry on your work: and in return I am going to ask you if you
would be so kind as to give me $50,000: Father owes the bank much
more: but if I had this much or even less: I know Mr. Bennett this
sounds like a lot of money for me to ask you for. but I feel that God
will richly bless you: I know you would not miss it. If you only
knew how badly he needed it. If you can possible see your way clear
to give me this amount as a gift. Will you please make the cheque
out to me as I do not want him to know that I asked you for
money: as you know one hates to take money: but I feel he needs
help right away; as the bank needs their money. I will work through
the manager of the Bank and help him: I do not know as there is
much more I can say, Mr. Bennett. It is rather hard to explain to one
in a letter: you always told me how nice looking I was last year: now
Mr. Bennett I have come to you for help: I do hope you will not

disappoint me: as it is the only chance I have to save my Father
from disaster. Please consider this letter as soon as possible: Hoping
to hear from you soon: I will be so grateful to you if you can help
me: I Remain Your Friend,

(Miss) Helene Arsten

[*A Conservative member of Parliament.]

397541-4

Toronto, Ontario
June 24th 1932

Sir:—
    Fulling realizing that the many problems created by present-day   ×××
conditions are so many and complex as to probably overwhelm any
one mortal in the position of first minister of the Crown. I am only
wondering if the problem of one Canadian returned soldier would be
of sufficient interest to the Prime Minister as to merit a few minutes
of his time to learn of them, and perhaps, of his courtesy, suggest
some action which might lead to a way out. If no other purpose is
served my difficulties might, in any case, give a close up of present
day conditions as they affect one Canadian family.
    I am 41 years of age, married, with 3 children, aged 8, 5 and 3
years respectively. My own parentage is Canadian, U.E.L. stock,
Welland County, the family being pioneers in the neighborhood of
Thorold. I was born in Waterloo, public school education in
Waterloo and Toronto; High School to matriculation in 1907 in
Winnipeg. When I entered the C.N.R. Freight Department at
Winnipeg as Junior, stenographer, secretary to Mr. T.J. Macdonald,
and rate clerk, leaving in 1911 to go to the Canadian Pacific Railway
as Chief Rate Clerk, where I remained until December, 1912, when I
returned to Toronto to engage in a small electrical contracting and
supply business, which I was forced to relinquish on my enlistment
in February 1916 in the 116th Canadian Inf. Bn. (Ontario County).

I enlisted as private, serving under Lt. Col. Sam Sharpe, (deceased) and served in his regiment in England, France and Belgium until Jan. 2, 1918, transferring to the 6th Bn. C.R.T., returning to Canada for discharge on June 16th, 1919, a service of 3 years and 4 months.

On my return I had to find a job, and first served as a placement officer with the Dept. of Soldiers Civil Re-establishment for a short time only and for a couple of years I worked variously in Ontario and Northern New York State. Suffering I suppose from the usual returned soldiers' difficulty of settling down after the upheaval and the wreckage of all fixed ideas by the war. However I finally settled down in Toronto in 1923, as Accountant for a large American Corporation, and was married. Shortly thereafter this firm closed their Canadian Branches and I went with the H.B.Gans Co. Limited of Baden in their Toronto Branch, first as salesman, and latterly as District Sales Manager. This firm, due to conditions, were forced to discontinue in September, 1930, when I found myself with a wife and 3 young children, and no job. Since that time, through various selling possitions on a commission we managed to eke out our existence until February of this year, when we were finally forced to apply for food to the Toronto Relief authorities. Since February I have had 3 days City Relief work as a laborer, 2 days relief work as a laborer on the addition to the local Parliament Buildings earning in Cash $21.60 and also some relief work for the local Poppy Fund which took care of rent and gas bills, etc. to the extend of $70.00, which they paid direct. We haven't a cent, are dependent on the City for our food, (which *does not* provide proper nourishment for a young family), are 4 months behind with out rent and are apparently up against a blank wall. As you will have gathered, in addition to being a stenographer and bookkeeper, I am also a fairly well trained executive. Experience has shown me that I am perhaps not fit for labour work without injury to my health, but I can do it. There are no positions available in the papers these days in my own line. I have applied for scores without result. It was suggested by an official of the Ontario Government who is a friend that I should apply for a temporary position with the Govt (Provincial) in connection with their relief programme. This I did to Hon. W.G.Martin, being supported by Mr. Rigg, Dominion Govt. Director of Employment, who served in France with me. One letter from Mr. Martin referred me to Hon. J.D.Monteith (Public Works and Labor) and a later one stated, that while nothing was known as to plans my letter would be kept on file. Dept. of Public Works replied to the same effect.

I do not infer, Sir, that my difficulties are in any sense your problem. Were I alone I should take my medicine without a whimper, but what of my kiddies? My father, in the undisturbed pursuit of life, liberty and happiness was able to create, provide for and fairly well educate a family of 6. Out of that 6, I was, while nicely started on the way to an established private business, uprooted, my whole aspect changed, and 3½ highly productive years spent in service with the C.E.F. After I get settled down again, marry and have the kiddies come along, during which process very little more can be done than get a footing toward re-establishment, this commercial upheaval comes along. Frankly after nearly two years of nerve wracking struggle and privation, only to land in absolute destitution is it any wonder that one is desperate. Is this what we fought for? that the man who will gladly sink education, experience, pride and everything he values to work in any menial capacity at any return which will provide the necessities of life for his family, food, shelter and clothing, cannot, despite superhuman efforts, find even that consolation. What kind of a chance are my children to get, even compared to the life equipment the average citizen of the past generation gave us. If this is all, then it were manifestly better that their father had gone west over there, or take the same road as my old C.O., Colonel Sam took. I dont value my war service. I always felt that if a country was fit to live in it was fit to fight for without question. I didnt expect bonuses, gratuities, or anything of that nature. Even army pay was never a factor. I never felt anything was due to me. It was the plain duty of a citizen who was free from family ties and his responsibility just as fixed as taxes. But *now What?* That is what I cant get away from. Doesn't Canada owe me the right to earn a living? Am I to continue in charitable slavery until the last vestige of morale is gone, and my family and their chance for happiness destroyed? Toronto Poppy Fund, where I might have earned payment for a little rent, etc. is bankrupt. Christie St Hospital—(Dept of Pensions & National Health) is only open to assist pensioners. Although a life long supporter of Conservative policies I have never been an active party worker, and as a consequence it is apparent I am not to be considered even for a temporary appointment in handling the Government Relief Programme. Two applications in response to Ottawa Civil Service Advertisements both resulted first in an acknowledgement, and latterly a statement that while returned soldiers got the preference, disabled returned pensioners got first preference. I am not critical of this regulation, but again what about me and my "Young Canadians"?

Platitudes in the Press about "World Wide Condition", "Canada is Solvent", etc etc ad infinitum only leave this problem unsolved and our personal condition daily growing more hopeless and more critical. *And*—had there been no war—what then—is it not an even chance that my little business carried on aggressivley would by this time have been yielding perhaps more than a competence. Anyhow— I wouldn't mind that if I could *earn a living* for them *now.* I dont suppose there is any answer. It will be just a case of down, down, and further down to the point from which I fear there will be no getting back, because it will be too late, and for them, poor kids, the valuable formative time of their lives will have been soured and spoiled. If you can tell me of an answer, Mr. Prime Minister, then you will be indeed an Oracle.

This letter is written with deepest respect to yourself, your high office, and the many difficulties which beset your path in these troublous times. I apologize for its length and can only add in explanation, that I felt compelled to write it.

Yours very truly
F. Deane

[Reply]

Ottawa, August 3, 1932.

Dear Mr. Deane:
I have kept before me your letter of the 24th of June in the hope that I might be able to have your attention directed to some vacancy where your services could be utilized.

I read your letter with more than ordinary concern and you are apparently facing the difficulties which confront you with very great courage. Government positions are practically all under the control

of the Civil Service Commission, but it seems to me you would be
well advised to write to the Secretary of the Commission and ask
him if there are any positions available for which you would be
eligible.

I would be very glad to bring your qualifications to the attention
of any companies with which I felt there was a chance of your
securing a position, but at the present time most companies have
been compelled to dispense with the services of valued employees,
and it is therefore difficult for me to be of assistance to you.

I do hope it may be possible for you to secure a position that will
enable you to give to your family the benefits that they require.

I trust you will accept my apology for the long delay in writing
you. The truth is I have been very greatly pressed with work in
connection with the Conference. If at any time you think I can be of
service to you, please do not hesitate to write me.

Yours faithfully,
R.B.Bennett

394878-87

Fairview, N.S.
July 20/32

Premier R B Bennet
Ottawa

Dear Mr. Bennet
I am taking the privilege in writing you this letter as I am a young
lady inwhich is having bad luck. So I thought it would be know
harm to write you and explain matters to you. My father has never
worked since Feb and with this terrible depression I am scared we
are going to loose our home we have a mortgage of $1000 and we
can not pay the payments and live. So I thought when I seen your
picture in the paper and so much about you It would be no harm to
ask you. Would you be so kind to lend me $75.00 we owe $70.00 of

payments on that arrears of $70.00 and if we dont get that in short
they will close the mortgage and take the house from us. So if you
would kindly lend me that amount I will give you a $100.00 fur for
Security. Untill I make ends meet to pay you back. I do not want to
Sell the fur as it was a gift to me. But if I can help my father out in
any way I must try and do it. As he is all that my sister and I owns
and my sister isn't strong. We where very well of in our day but my
father invested all his money in a coal mine and lost it all and then
this terrible depression came and we had to put a mortgage of $1000
on our home its awful when we where always well of only for Mr.
Eastman who has the mortgage of our house we would be swept out
a month ago but he took pity on us and he is trying to give me a
chance to get the payments we have to pay $10.00 per month and
we owe seven months payments so if you will help me out God will
put stars in your crown I do not want this depression to down me as
I am a staunch Concerative Tory to the bone. If I get this mortgage
payments paid I will be a happy girl then I intend to try and make
ends meet by doing cooking for people I am enclosing letters so you
will know I am telling you the truth I am sorry to bother you when
you are so busy but I am in such a way I dont know what to do I
dont want to loose my home. I am a good living girl. Hoping that
you will help me out.

Your's Lovingly
Miss E.L. Glean

My mother is dead she died with Cancer.

397643-6

Koradaska P. Office, Quebec
Aug 26th/32

Mr Bennett.
Dear Sir,
    Just a few lines to let you know that I had a baby boy the Second
of June & I am calling him Richard Bennett & I want you to send
him a little token as we have eight of a family & my husband can't
get work & we are in a ma____ Starving to death. as you know we
always vote conservicer & this election our oldest son will have a
vote & I hope the Lord will be with you in all you say & do if you
will help the poor in need. hoping to hear from you soon I remain
Your loving Friend,

Mrs. James M. McKevin

[Reply: Mr Bennett sent a cup from Calgary.]

75505

Alberta
Oct 29th 32

Hon R.B.Bennett
Ottawa,

Sir
    We have lost three lives in this provence in the last two weeks,
one a father of three children, killed in the Calder railway yards, it is
charged by some that He was knocked off a car by one of the police,
when He was trying to get aride to get home to His family, the other
was a case of murder near manvell, of a elevator opperator, when
also 600 dollars was taken, it is thought some transent likely did this
murder, perhaps to get money to pay his fare home, another farmer
Was murdered and money taken, Do you think Your action in order-
ing, that theses poor fellows should be denied a free ride on a freight

after the 15th of September,* had anything to do theses sad deaths,
if so on whome will the blood rest, and who should take care of the
wives and the poor little children, think it over and act quickly, that
they may not suffer more than the have already. In as much as ye
did it unto one of the least & etc.

Yours truly
one who feels deeply for theses
poor people and am as poor.

[*A reference to a government edict denying free rides on freights to
stranded unemployed. Previously the practice had been winked at
and often encouraged by local officials.]

490922

Port Lieu, Quebec
Nov. 2nd/32

To Mr Bennett. P.M. of Can.
Ottawa, Canada.

Dear Sir,
    We are a family of nine persons that has lost everything we had
by fire with no insurance & since the depression we are very desolate
to see that we are in want of everything, provision but more
especially clothing for which I come to implore your kindness &
good-will before the cold weather sets in for the following list of
clothing for to dress my family I would be very thankful to you if
you would send these clothes to my adress to Port Lieu station &
not to the Sec-Tres of the council for half the time we dont see the
glimpse of it or what we get is very scant. I am in great need of it &
hoping that you will grant me this favor—

I am Y. V. Sincerely—
Michael Raymond Jones

List of clothing that we need the most—

	sizes
6 prs Mens Underwear	36 & 38
3 " " Pants	32
3 " Sweaters	36 & 38
3 " " Rubber Boots	8. 8. 9
4 " Women Underwear	36 & 38
4 Womens dresses	36
2 " Sweaters	36
2 prs womens felt boots	5
1 " girls " "	12
2 girls underwear	9 yrs
4 Boys Underwear	12 & 8 yrs
2 " Sweaters	12 & 8 yrs
2 " Suits	12 & 8 yrs
2 " rubber boots	12 & 2

394194-6

Wolten, Sask.,
Nov. 10th 1932

Right Hon. Mr. Bennett.

Dear Sir:—

Winter is here and once more I think of skating, but being such hard times and Mother and Dad are poor and the bit of money I earned in the holidays had to go on clothes for winter.

All the other boys are skating and I think I could skate as good as most of them if I could get a pair of skates, second hand or new about size seven.

School is going to be closed for the biggest part of this winter and there will be nothing else to do but sit and watch them enjoy themselves. I was thinking of this and then I thought of our Premier and

thought that you might suggest some means for me to get enough
for a pair of skates.

Yours sincerely
Piet Hanson

[Reply]

Ottawa, December 12, 1932

Dear Sir:
    In response to the appeal contained in your letter of November
10th, I am enclosing, by Mr. Bennett's direction, five dollars, which I
think will cover the cost of a skating outfit.

Yours faithfully,
Private Secretary

396641, 396643

C.B. Berkley & Company, Limited
Wholesale and Retail General Merchants
Trafalgar, B.C. Nov. 16th, 1932

Hon. R.B.Bennett,
Ottawa, Ont.

Dear Mr. Bennett:
    About two years ago, if you remember, I discussed with you the
financial position of my firm, and if I remember correctly, showed
you our financial statement which was at that time pretty bad.
Needless to say, the last two years of depression have made our
position very much worse, and I have just about come to the end of
my tether. I do not think that I can last through the winter. I have
been fighting for all that is in me, but I am afraid that I am beaten.

I have no money and if the business is forced to close, I will be in a very bad way. I have been wondering if the Government has any position to offer that I could fill. I have been in business from early boyhood, first with my father then with W.H.Turner & Company, St. John, N.B., afterwards in British Columbia. I have mixed with all kinds of people in a business way from the highest to the lowest, and I am not afraid to tackle any position that required business ability. My health is splendid for which I am devoutly thankful. In fact, I never was so well in my life. Should there be any position open, or to be open, which I am able to fill, I would be very grateful if you would keep me in mind. Everything I have in earth is tied up in my business and so far as I can see there is no hope of pulling it out.

I want to take this opportunity to congratulate you on the success of the Imperial Conference in Ottawa. I feel sure great benefits will come to Canada through the agreements made with the different units of our Empire and I think they will have the effect of binding the Empire closer together. I was very pleased and thankful that the Conference was so successful.

Thanking you for any consideration that you may give to my request,

I am,
Yours truly,
C.B. Berkley

397077

Campbellton, N.B.
Nov. 29, 1932

Dear frend
I am taking the plasure in rinting you a few lines to ask you if you would healp me out in some way for I am sick and I can[t] work and the Dotor wount halp me out in anny way witeout money I toat you would halp me wite a treaman for I tink you are the onny one would

halp me out for I vouted for you so trie to halp me out some way
and I will never for get you I am yours very truly Rufus snider.

397680

Harney Sask
Nov 30 1932

Dear Mr Bennett.
    I just thought I would write to you Because I thought you would
write Santa for me and tell him I was a good girl all the time. and
Mamma tells me her and Daddy has no money to give Santa for my
little brother and me and we cant hang up our stockings up. Would
you send me some money and I will send it to him or do you think
Mr Bennett he would forget Brucy and me my I hope he dont I wish
you write and tell him Im here and Imll be so good. but if Daddy has
no money to give him he can't come. Will you write and tell me if
you wrote to Santy.

I will close now
Dody Brandt

[Reply: $3.00.]

400736

Ottawa
Ont.
Nov. 30th. 32

Dear Sir
    I hope you will excuse me taken this liberty in writing to you. I
know your time is taken up with more important things than this
but when I saw in the papers that you were going away I was
desperate. Ive been going to write often, but I could not seem to get
up enough courage. Well sir, my story is this. I've sat many nights
alone wondering if there was anything in life. But I think there must
be happiness some were yet for my little girl and me. Sir I have the
lovliest little girl 10 years old and she's all the world to me. Ive had
an awfull life for the last 13 years but sickness etc. have kept me
here Ime married but after all he's my little girls father and I dont
want to say anything All I want sir is to go away quietly some were
with my little girl and try and earn a living for us both. I dont want
to have no trouble. Ime desperate or I would not appeal to you. I
have not a cent to go any place were I could make a start for us. And
our clothes are not suitable. Ime only asking for a loan as I shall pay
every cent back. I have read lots about your kindness and oh sir its
not much I ask for but it would mean a little bit of heaven for us
both. We could be so happy away together from all this. I know I
could work for us. I know you must be busy preparing for your trip
and you must have lots of demands made on you But I hope you
can spare a little of your time to read this. If I could only get enough
to start us. I dont make many friends. I keep my troubles to myself.
Your the first one I ever wrote to But Xmas is so near and I should
like to spend a little happier one than last year. You do not know
what I have suffered. I hope you will excuse me being so bold as to
write to you. But oh I just had to do something. And please excuse
any mistakes ive made as this is the first time ive wrote to a Prime
Minister. I shall ask God to bless you allways and work my fingers
off to pay you back. If I left here I'd let you know if you wished it

my address right away allow me to wish you sir a happy holiday.

I am Yours respectfully
(Mrs) Henrietta Brown

P.S. I have to have my letters sent to here as ime afraid to have them
sent home

[Reply: $5.00.]

400730-4

St Leon Val Racine
16 janvier 1933

Bien cher honorable Monsieur Benett
     Je vous ecrie cert quelque mots pour vous demande de me venir
en aider car je suis dans le besoin je croi que si sa continue que
nous allont mourrir de fin   je vous demande cela parceque jai bou-
coup travaille pour vous dans le tent des élection   jai travaille pour
vous et je suis près a n'en faire encore autent et vous le verrai au
prochaine élection   je suis marie et jai cinq petit enfants et jai pas
d'ouvrage et je veut travailler   si vous aviez quelque chose pour moi
je suis près a tout faire   si vous aviez comme par exemple une joob
ofisier raporteur sur nimportequelle jenre, je suis près a travaille pour
vous et pour notre beau canada   vous verrai au prochaine election   je serai pas le dernier a vous serrai la main et a me faire
aconaitre parmie vos bon citoyens du canada   jai toujours été pour
vous un hiro du canada et encore ont a des discute contre vous et je
peut me battre pour vous   je vous demande de bien vouloir m'aide
de nimporte quel maniére la manier qui vous plaira et au prochaine
election vous verrai dans St Leon Val Racine que sa sera tout pour
vous et envoyer moi des écriture pour prouvie ce que vous avez fait
pour nous   nos bon Libereaux ne voulent pas cela eux autres faite

pour moi ce que je doublerai pour vous   s'il vous plait de votre
devoué serviteur

Mrs. M.S. Hubert

394198-9

Ferguson, N.B.
March 21, 1933

Hon. R.B.Bennett
Ottawa, Can.

Dear Sir,
    The respectable people of this country are *fed up* on feeding the
bums for that is all they can be called now. This "free" relief (free to
the bums) has done more harm than we are altogether aware of. The
cry of those who get it is "Bennett says he wont let anyone starve".
They don't consider that the *people* (many poorer than themselves
but with more spunk) have to foot the bill. The regulations (which
are only a poor guide after all) were too loose from the start and
could be and *were* easily side stepped many times.
    Getting relief has become such a habit that the majority think
only of how to get it regularly instead of trying to do without once
in a while. Nearly all of them have dogs too which are fed by
the country and are of no practical use. One family near me has
three and another has two and others one and I know it is the same
everywhere. I also know that food enough to keep one dog will keep
at least four hens and keep them laying. The family that has the
three dogs ate at least 550 pounds of meat from the second week in
November until the first part of March. There are the parents, twins
10 years old and four children from one year to eight. Who but the
dogs got a good part of that? Also dogs everywhere are chasing and
catching deer but if a man tries to get one for the family he is either
fined or jailed if found out. Or if he tries to get a few fish (he is
mighty lucky if he succeeds above Newcastle on the Miramichi now)

the wardens are right after him and he finds himself minus a net at
the least.

Now the taxes are going to be forcibly collected to pay for the
good-for-nothings for whom the debt was made. Those people
should be made work and there wouldn't need to be much forcing
for taxes. The taxpayers don't consider that they should keep people
as well and sometimes better off than they are and their wives agree
with them. We see plainly now that those being kept will not help
themselves so long as they are fed for nothing.

Notice should be given at once to enable them to get crops in and
so on and relief stopped altogether. The cost of that would pay for a
good deal of work. Also please remember there are other people in
the country who need your thought as well as those on relief as it is
now though they are struggling along somehow. I think it only fair
to state that if it continues or is considered for the future there will
be a goodly number of Conservatives vote the other way for as I
stated in the beginning we are sick and tired of being forced to keep
the majority that are following the relief path. It hasn't been fair all
through as any thoughtful man must know. I am not stating this idly
because I have talked with many others many times and that is the
general feeling. I think I can safely say too that the Liberals getting
relief don't thank the Conservatives enough to give them a vote
either because they nearly all say the country owes them a living and
think no thanks are due.

I could write more but will let this suffice for this time but Please
consider this question of relief as a very important one because a
deal of trouble may brew from it.

Yours respectfully,
Mrs. Ernest Ferguson

481832-4

Calgary May 1/33

Hon. R.B.Bennett Esq.
Ottawa

Dear Sir,
   I am a young man unemployed wishing to get back to England, is there anyway of doing so.
   I am a liability on the Dominion having been on Relief for 4 years Am willing to work my way over if there is the opportunity of doing so. Would you kindly let me know if anything can be done in the matter please. Wishing you the best of health and a successful term of Office.

Yours Sincerely
R.H. Stephen

76598

May 20, 1933
Calgary, Alberta

Rt. Hon. R.B.Bennett,
Ottawa, Can.

We came to the great West and located in Edmonton in 1906. Our eldest son was born in Edmonton in 1910. With the exception of one year spent in N.S. we have lived in Calgary the remainder of the time. Our second son was born in April 1914, just before the war started. Our only daughter born in 1917.
   During the war there was no building (my husband is a carpenter) and we had built a home here and bought some building lots. We met the situation by exchanging places. I went teaching school and my husband looked after the boy, then only six months old. After a long time my husband secured some work at small pay and I was able to stay at home but substituted in the city schools.

Our eldest son finished High School but we could not send him to the University. Our second son is last year in High School. Notwithstanding the fact that we have worked so hard—have clear title to two houses—we are not able to help our boys and they cannot get work to help us. We rent one place at Twenty Two dollars a month and live in the other. Our taxes to the city are nearly Two Hundred Dollars besides the general taxes every month. Our idea in acquiring property was to have an income for our later years. If things do not change very soon, we shall lose what we have. It is a nightmare to think of it as my husband worked night and day to build these homes, even holidays were spent in this manner.

My husband belongs to the Cameron clan (whose parents made homes for them in the forests of N.S.) and my people are United Empire Loyalist descendants. Can you imagine what the present conditions are doing to people of our pride?

Our sons have good habits, they are strong, sensible and practical all they want is a chance to do.

My husband is getting some work but it is very hard work and small pay. He works whether sick or well, often not able to eat any breakfast. The rental from our house pays the monthly bills; what my husband earns runs the table but you see there is nothing left to pay taxes. Then if my husband does not get any work as he cannot have it much longer, what are we going to do. Remember, we are doing our best and there may be many more like us but not many who have worked so hard.

I had piano pupils in the good times but many cannot pay any longer.

Is it true that gold may be increased in value and our purchasing power reduced? We want to see the Douglas System* established in Alberta. We sincerely hope your government will not do anything against it.

I take this privilege of writing you as I had the very great honor of conferring with you on an important topic during the war, through a letter from J.Ed.MacDonald, Bart. of Pictou, N.S.

After having studied, listened, planned and schemed, I am writing to you as a last resort to try to do something to increase the purchasing power of the people. I have been wondering if I could write a book or some short stories to earn something but I am too worried and have so much work looking after the family and studying economics.

Trusting you will not think too harshly of me for writing this, I remain, Yours in difficult difficulties.

(Mrs.) Sarah M. Jones

[*Social Credit.]

[Reply]

Personal
Ottawa, May 27th, 1933

Dear Mrs. Jones,

I have before me your letter of recent date and I have read with sympathetic interest the record of the endeavours of your husband and yourself to establish a home for your children. You appear to have worked very hard, and while the results at the moment are not what you seem to deserve, I am certain you will continue to do your best to maintain the home you have secured.

I am fully aware of conditions as they now exist, and the Federal Government is making every possible effort for the purpose of bettering the conditions of our people. I think there is now an upturn in conditions generally, and we will continue to direct all our efforts towards ever increasing improvement.

I had hoped that it might be possible to go to Calgary for a few days before leaving for the World Conference, but in view of the fact that the House has not yet prorogued, I find that is now impossible. Had I been able to go West, I would have made arrangements to see you and have a few words with you with regard to the situation about which you have written.

You have faced the past with great courage and there is little doubt from the terms of your letter but that you will face the future with the same spirit, so that with the improvement of conditions in

this country, you may look forward to being rewarded for the
efforts you have made.

Yours faithfully,
R.B.Bennett

79480-4

Winnipeg, Manitoba
June 8th, 1933

Hon. R.B.Bennett
Ottawa, Ont.

Dear Sir:—
    Sometime ago I wrote a letter to you appealing for help or
employment.
    It is now forty months since I had the pleasure of a pay check.
    My family, are all undernourished, ill clothed and ill sheltered and
are in need of Medical Assistance.
    How long do you think we can carry on under these
circumstances.
    You stated that there would be no one starve in Canada I
presume you meant not starve over night but slowly our family
amongst thousands of others are doing the same slowly and slowly.
    Possibly you have never felt the Pang of a Wolf. Well become a
Father have children then have them come to you asking for a slice
of bread between meals and have to tell them to wait. Wait until five
of humanitys humans sleep all in one room no larger than nine
square feet with one window in it.
    My previous letters, have explained all and further explaination is
not necessary.
    After a fashion my previous letters are just so much paper with
words of a meaningless nature to you regardless to what it has meant
to my family.
    I want work of a nature that will provide an honest living Now

not ten years from now.

I am not radical, Red or unloyal but I would appreciate an honest chance in this world for my family.

I do not believe I am crazy but am reaching the breaking point.

My body, my muscles, my brain are like sodden wood crumbling under this strain. Though the lack of idleness.

I have knowledge of Electrical work—Chaffeur—Sailor— Telephone and Telegraph work.

For God's sake please make a personal endeavour to assist me toward a brighter outlook immediately

Yours Very Sincerely
Charles Grierson

[See also letters from Grierson on pp. 22, 68, 151, 156, 161, 172.]

396056-9

St. Philemon, Quebec
24 Juin 1933

A monsiur R B Banette
Monsiur Je ne vousdra pas vous deplaire avec se petit tapis   Je ne vous envois pas cela pour vous dire que je suis en moyans non sa sera tous le contraire Monsiur   je suis a la charite de la parroise et mon marie est malade incapable de travailer voila quelque anne   et jais 7 enfants sur les bras tous a bas âge   je vous envois ce tapis comme souvenir et pour vous montre quon sera encore pour vous comme on na été pour le passé.

Mad Charles Leseigneur

escusé mois

396656

Calgary, Alberta
August 24th, 1933

Hon: R.B.Bennett,
Ottawa.

Dear Sir,
I hardly know how to begin, but in desperation I am appealling to
you as a brother in masonary.
I have heard the Fraters speak of you, and as I have been a
member of Al Azhar Temple since 1914, a Shriner who knew you
most intimately, who was also a lawyer, said you were the most
humane, most kindly man he knew, so, on that assumption I am
taking courage to write to you.
My crop is entirely gone, the garden also, and I haven't one thing
to sell, and my wife is very sick. Last October she came up to
Calgary for medical advice, as she was very sick. She has a tumor,
and as she has some terrible hommorhages which made her very
anemic, an operation was inadvisable. As the tumor was quite large
and might become malignant, radium treatments were given. Her
tonsils were removed as the poison had gone to her throat, so I have
had to keep her in Calgary. She was in the hospital here in Calgary
for a little while, but I have been looking after her, to save the cost
of a nurse. As you are aware the past three years have been very
trying for farmers and ranchers. The price of products being below
the cost of production, so with sickness also I have no money. Last
week I enquired about relief. It takes courage, and courage of the
bravest kind to ask for relief. I have been humiliated and sent from
pillar to post, just as if I were a criminal or something. I have lived
on my farm, or ranch in the old days for over 30 years, 31 years
next March to be exact. Was the first man in Alberta to raise a 50
bushel crop of wheat (in 1906). Have paid taxes all that time, have
helped several hundred people and yet, when I am frantic with
despair what happens? We have not lived long enough in the city for
relief, residing here not quite a year, A fellow Shriner told me to put
my pride in my pocket and go to the Mounted Police Barracks here,
which I did, they informed me I should be here a year at least before
they could do anything, so I was sent back to the farm, to the
municipality. They also wanted to "pass the buck" as we had resided

in Calgary since last October. As I knew the men in charge a good many years they did fill in a form but they can't call a council for at least two or three weeks. For my wife's sake I am asking you to help me obtain relief so that I can get it here. Only the most dire necessity would have induced me to apply for it. There is also the children, two whom are of school age, 12 and 14 years of age. My wife has been ordered, milk, beefsteak, orange juice, etc., also some certain medicines. She must build her strength up. I don't want to see her die by inches before my eyes.

Please forgive me taking up so much of your valuable time, but I am desperate and almost insane from worry. I am,

Your's fraternally,
Noah Norris

77210-1

Toronto. Sept. 3/33

Hon. R.B.Bennett.

Dear Sir,
I am writing to you because I am in desperate straits. I am not a beggar nor am I a person of nerve, but I am about to lose my home. I have paid $3300.00 in it and now the mortgage company will foreclose unless I can pay up all that is owing this month. I have three sons, aged 17, 19 and 21, all so willing and anxious to work but can get absolutely nothing at all to do to earn a dollar, they have tried to get in the Camps* but have been refused because they have a home in the city, or because they were unfortinate enough to be born in Toronto. I was born in Nova Scotia but have lived here over twenty five years. Yet I must lose all, is there no way, is there not anything that can be done. I am told that I am only one in thousands. does that better my position any? I am forty seven years old and have worked hard for everything I ever had, and it is hard to see it go now.

Mr. Bennett, I believe you to be a good as well as a great man,
therefore I am apealing to you to help me save my home. picture
yourself, through no fault of your own, homeless. with sons willing,
but unable to provide for you.

Mr. Bennett. could you help me by a loan of five hundred dollars.
I know times will be better as I realize you are striving toward that
very thing as best you can and your great efforts will bring success,
but my need is now.

Please help me or what can I do.

Trusting you will be our esteemed Priemer for many years, I
remain

Yours Sincerely and hopefully.
(Mrs) Laura Bates

[*Work camps for homeless, single, unemployed men were established in 1932 by the Department of National Defence. See the
introduction.]

[Reply]

Ottawa,
8th September, 1933.

Mrs. Laura Bates
Toronto, Canada.

Dear Madam,–

I regret very much to learn of your unfortunate circumstances, as
stated in your letter of September 3rd.

I too have suffered to some extent from the existing economic
conditions. I have endeavoured to assist others so far as was
reasonably possible but I cannot hope to meet the many requests
made upon me.

I am certainly willing to try to help you and if you will be good
enough to let me know what company holds the mortgage on your

home I will look into the matter and see if anything can be done to
straighten out the difficulties.

Yours faithfully,
R.B.Bennett

396681-4

Sept 18 1933
St John N.B.

Hon. R.B.Bennett
Ottawa Can.

Dear Sir:—

I got a man here boarding at my house of 60 yrs old he is single
and last winter he applied at the relief office to Mr Roderick Kearns
the relief director but he was refused assistance so I kept him at my
house hoping that he would get some work now its over 3 months
that I am boarding him and I have run a big Bill with my grocer that
I am unable to pay because my husband is not working.

Now I want you to send me one dollar a day for keeping this man
since the 12th of May he had no work and he was out in the road. its
worth that to board a man and wash his cloths. his name is Philippe
Raymond.

Yours truly
Mrs David Barbeau

481746

Wesley Ont.,
Sept. 27, 1933

The Hon. R.B.Bennett
Parliament Building
Ottawa, Ontario

Dear Sir:
    In August of this year, Three Little Baby Boys were born to Mr.
and Mrs. Samuels in our vicinity.
    The parents are English, but a very fine type, not the kind with
the hand out for help.
    Like many others, they have had some very bad luck. They
worked for a farmer whose daughter has come home and brought
her family and husband. That left them without work or home.
    Mr. and Mrs Samuels are both staunch Conservatives. So I asked
them to give the triplets good names. The largest one was called,
Warner Bennett, the next was Russell Ferguson,* and the third
Donald Henry.*
    These parents are without friends or relatives in this country, we
feel that these little chaps should have their chance in life.
    The Mother and Babies are still in Hospital, expecting to be able
to leave the end of the month. The People of Wesley have asked
them to make their home here for awhile at least.
    We hope that you will feel toward these unfortunate people as
we do.

Yours truly,
Elizabeth Rattray

[*Howard Ferguson and George Henry were successive Conservative
premiers of Ontario.]

[Reply]

Ottawa, December 13, 1933

Dear Mr. and Mrs. Samuels
    I am enclosing herewith a $20 bill, which I trust may be of some
little service to you during the Christmas season in securing some gift
for your little boy, whom you were good enough to name after me.
    I learned the other day that one of the triplet boys had passed
away, and I extend to you my sincerest sympathy. I trust the other
little boys are in good health.
    With best wishes, believe me, I am

Yours faithfully,
R.B.Bennett

396994, 396999

Kingdom, Sask.
Sept 28 1933

Prime Minister R.B.Bennette
Ottawa Ont

Dear Sir it is with a very humble heart I take the opportunity of
writing this letter to you to ask you if you will please send for the
underware in the Eaton order made out and enclosed in this letter
My husband will be 64 in Dec. and his nuritis very bad at times in his
arms and shoulders. We have had very little crop for the last three
years: not enough at all to pay taxes and live and this year crops
around here (West of Saskatoon) are a complete failure. My husband
is drawing wood on the waggon for 34 miles., and had to draw hay
too, for feed for horses this winter. He has to take two days for a
trip, and sleep out under the waggon some times. He is away for
wood today and it is cold and windy. So I am writing this in the

hope that you will send for this underware, as we really have not the
money ourselves. I have patched & darned his old underware for the
last two years, but they are completely done now, if you cant do
this, I really dont know what to do. We have never asked for anything of anybody before, We seem to be shut out from the world
altogether we have no telephone Radio or newspaper. For this last
couple of years we have felt we could not afford to have them. We
used to enjoy your speeches on the Radio also the Sunday Church
Services, as we cant get out very much in winter. if I can only get
this underware for my husband I can manage for myself in some
way. He has to be out in the cold, where I can stay in the house, for
the truth of this letter I refer you to Rev. J.B. Jackson, Paster.
United Church. Kingdom or Dr. A.J. Portens M.D. Saskatoon Sask.
    Thanking you in advance I remain yours truly

Mrs Thomas Perkins
Kingdom Sask

[Reply]

Personal & Confidential
Ottawa, October 7, 1933.

Dear Madam:
    I have before me for acknowledgment your letter of the 28th of
September directed to the Prime Minister.
    While you can realize Mr. Bennett has been inundated with
similar requests, nevertheless in view of the health of your
husband I have forwarded to the T.Eaton Co. Limited, order for
high grade, heavyweight Wolsey underwear, which I trust you will
receive in due course.
    I trust you will treat this matter as strictly confidential.

Yours faithfully,
Secretary.

396174-7

[Reply]

Kingdom Nov 15/33

Prime Minister R.B.Bennett.

Dear Sir received your kind favor of underware for my husband. We wish to thank you very very much for it. It was a whole month from you forwarded the order to Eatons, untill we received it. but we sure are thankful to you for your kindness

Mr & Mrs Thos Perkins

396182

Mr. Walter A. Jensen
St John N.B.
12/10/1933

My Honorable Sir
    Just a few lines in Regards to present day life and also that in Which we live in as one that served King and Country for almost five years overseas in the Navy I find myself in a trying time. I am Serving now the King of Kings and I am pleased to Inform your Honorable Sir that in all our ways it pays to call upon the Lord and He Will leads us through. So Sir I am through Our Lord Jesus Christ asking you to consider we return Men that are without a pension and also debared of Medical Aid and we have little ones to care for this Coming Winter and living on Starvesion relief which is not enough to Keep ones body soul mind and Spirit together. The Lord Knows How we Shall overcome praying that the Lord may open up your Hearts to give to the poor and needy their needs remember time is Short and Eturnity Nigh God Shall Judge the World in righteousness by that man who he hath Ordained whereoff He Hath give Asurance

Unto all men in that He hath raised Him from the dead So praying
the Lord will help You to believe His Word it is more blessed to give
then it is to receive praying the Blessings from God the father and
the Son and of the Holy Spirit be your reward now and forever more
in the Name of Jesus. Mistic

481755-6

Passman Sask.
Oct 16th/33

Dear Sir, — I am a girl thirteen years old and I have to go to school
every day its very cold now already and I haven't got a coat to put
on. My parents can't afford to buy me anything for this winter. I
have to walk to school four and a half mile every morning and night
and I'm awfully cold every day. Would you be so kind to sent me
enough money to so that I could get one.
My name is

Edwina Abbott

[Reply: $5.00.]

396901

Faro, Alta.
Oct 30/33

Mr. R.B.Bennett
Prime Minister of Canada
Ottawa.

Dear Sir:—
    You will think it odd to receive a letter from a poor guy like me
asking the Prime Minister of Canada to do him a favour, but can

not help it, as present condition are such that a man can hardly
make a living on a farm, especially in the Peace River country. I am a
homesteader about one & a half mile from Northstand siding on the
Northern Alberta Railway. My crop was frozen & will not realize
very much out of same. I wrote to the manager of the Northern
Alberta Railway Co. at Edmonton for a small tie contract this
winter, did not yet receive a reply & its been two months since I
wrote.

   I am mighty hard up & have four children to keep in food &
clothing. I do not wish to go on releave, as never before in my life
have I been on releave, so I am asking you to do me a favour by
using your influence to induce the Northern Alberta Railway Co. to
let a poor homesteader like me have a small tie contract this winter,
in order to keep my family in food & clothing.

   You might ask your self who is this guy well I was born in
Medicine Hat forty two years ago. My dad was a good old consirvative ever since I can remember & ever since I had a vote, I voted
consirvative & always will. I do not know you personal but have
listened to your public speaches many a time.

   The other day after our school meeting, some one said; well Mr.
Bennett is at Calgary telling the unemployed what he has done
for them & they laughed, it sure made my blood boil. I told them
Mr. Bennett has done more for the unemployed than any other
Prime Minister could or have done in the present state of affairs the
whole world is in, we had it quite hot. I won out, as I never lay
down.

   I wish I could get more inside information as to what you have
done for Canada, in order to defend my self.

   Mr. Bennett you might think I am running a bluff, but it is the
Gods truth, I am for you every time.

   Hoping to hear from you before very long.

Yours Truly
F. Reznick

490201-3

Grimsby, Ont.
Nov. 3rd, 1933

Dear Sir, — Do you know it is just a fright here in Grimsby the way
the poor people are used, When they do get work from the farmers
which is not very often all they will pay is 10¢ an hr. But now it has
got so you can not get a job any wheres. The farmer's will offer a
married man to keep his family on all is 1¢ for picking up apples a
back, it has got to be something done as people can not live on that.
There has got to be relief given or work & better wages, because the
eats are up so high that a poor man can not afford it and something
has got to be done. And why not put some of these foreigners and
Indians in their own country & give a white man some show, as they
are taking the work away from the Canadian men and I would think
the Government could do something to prevent all of this. And the
people wander in Canada why so much robbing & bootlegging is
carried on. Now why is it? If we have any government at all. Why
not they look in to it as our Country is overrun by foreigners. By the
way they have to live and all of this way they have to carry on with.
If war does come the Dominion of Can. would be so week, She
wouldent be of much use.

486295-6

Chicago, 11/13/33

Dear Sir;—
    The enclosed letter* is my justification for addressing you at this
time on behalf of Mrs. Andrew Sanford of Toronto, daughter-in-law
of the late Sir George Sanford, at one time Prime Minister of
Canada.
    Mrs. Sanford is my half sister; she is very old and very ill. Her
income from *The Recorder,* a daily newspaper published in
Peterboro, Ont., has ceased within the last month, due to the
"depression" and Mrs. Sanford is on the verge of actual want. I am

an elderly widow myself and unable to aid Mrs. Sanford so,
unknown to her, I am bringing her unhappy plight to the attention
of her Government in the hope that *some* provision, however small,
may be made for her other than actual charity during the remaining
days of her life.

Yours very truly,
(Mrs.) Myra Francis Kirkmeyer

[*It has not been found.]

[Reply]

Personal
Ottawa, November 15, 1933

Dear Madam:
    Your letter of November 13th, addressed to my Secretary, is
before me.
    The case of Mrs. Sanford is but one of very many similar ones in
this country. We receive communications from the widows of
judges and Civil Servants, asking for assistance. This we are unable to
grant in any one case, for to do so would create a precedent and all
cases would have to be treated the same. For instance, the widow of
a late Chief Justice of Canada has presented very strong claims for
financial assistance in the way of an annuity or otherwise, but this
we are unable to grant.
    There is an Old Age Pension Act in force in the Province of
Ontario, under which Mrs. Sanford might be eligible for a pension,
or perhaps some of her friends or the personal friends of the late
Sir George Sanford might feel disposed to contribute to an annuity
for her. Outside of this, I know of no means by which your very
laudable desire to be of assistance to Mrs. Sanford could be gratified.

Yours faithfully,
R.B.Bennett

399159-61

McVittie Sask
Nov 22nd, 33

Premier Bennett
Ottawa

Dear Sir
    Haveing seen in the Regina Star. You express yourself well
pleased with the Optimistic Spirit shown by the People dureing
Your Western Trip. May I ask did you see any of the Western People
who have had *No Crops* for this last 4 or 5 years. I dout you did.
Because its utterly impossible with Overalls nearly dropping too
peices. Moleskin pants patched untill we do not know which is
patches or the original
    Do you think for one moment your Sister Mrs. Herredge would
feel very Optomistic if she was living under Conditions like that.
I say No. And its terrible things should be so. In a Country like this
So Rich in Natural Resources and in your own heart. You must
know that is absolutely true & should not be so. You men make all
kinds of Promises before you are Elected Break your Promises and
then you put *a Tax* on *Tea* & Sugar which should not be Aloowed
90 cents for 10 lbs of Granulated Sugar. How are we too live may I
ask under those Conditions. Thank God for the Mild & Beautiful
weather we are Haveing Just now or I am afraid there would be
more Severe Suffering And in black & white I saw that both you &
also Premier Anderson have repeatedly made the Statement from
Public Platforms that No Man, Woman, or Child should suffer
Privation in Saskatchewan or Canada this Winter
    We can of course Sympathize with a Harrased Government. And
we are willing to do all that lies in our power. But what can we do
when we cannot get Crops and such Poor Prices for our Produce 4
cents for a Doz Eggs
    My Hunsband was 64 May 22nd last I was 64 Nov 5th 1 year
older than you are Worked hard all our Lives. And Surely a little
Comfort should be comeing too us now. But how can we get 11
cents Butter Fat is all they are Paying 2 weeks ago So a Poor Widow
told us who is makeing a Brave Struggle under Conditions which
seem to getting Worse instead of Better
    You must know Mr Bennett the agony one endures too see how

we have and are trying too Pay our Taxes and Pay our Way Then
too be up against the Impossible. Of course you have not seen any of
our Sufferings during your Tour of The West. But God sees it and
He Knows Pardon me for speaking Plainly. But I see. No Diffirence
in your Party or The Liberal Party. You are Both High Tarriff. And
are put in by The Moneyed Men and also Dictated too by them. We
need more Miss Agnes McPhail's* in The Federal House & also in
Provincial House And we Certianly need *Less Government* for
10-000-000 People Taxes would not be so High then. And we are
trying so hard to pay our way Would not be nearly Taxed too Death
as we are now I used too think Mrs Pankhurst was A Foolish
Woman. I don't think so now She got what she set out for. Votes for
Women. Although I do not think window breaking was nice Glass is
too Dear. Costs too much When I see How these Hard Years Have
Affected My Husband, who has always been a Hardworking Man *I
am not Red.* But I see Red. And like *Many* More I ponder too
myself. Oh Lord how long How long What with the after effects of
the War. Which should never have been allowed and if those who
caused The War had been put in The Front Lines the War would
have been ended right then. The Moneyed Men are too blame for all
the Wars. Returned men did not even know what they had been
Fighting for Shrapnell Operations 2 or 3 and a peice left near the
Brain. And the Poor Fellow nearly went mad with the same thing.
Oh cruel cruel and The Capitalists Men are too Blame for The War. I
could tell you of lots of Cases and how I helped and did all I could
for that War from 1914 to 1918. But Never Again I would sooner be
killed myself, than too Think I had Helped Poor Fellows too Be
Maimed and Blinded in that way. But would Willingly Help too put
all those Responsible for War in The Front Line with Pleasure and
then there would be No War Would there We even have too Pay
towards Telephone and yet cannot Afford too have one Because we
Have So many Governments and so many Fighting for Seats That
there must be Something in it *For Them Worth While* We shall
Forget what Pears Grapes Rasps and Strawberries taste like soon 3 or
4 years without even seeing one 18 oranges in 2 years 12 or 15
Lemons & Tons of Stuff rotting in The Orchards both East & West If
We had a Good Government That would not be Allowed You in
Your Suite of 17 Rooms Furnished in Princly Style Beautiful Rugs
etc cannot *Understand* What We women Suffer with Old Slippers

and Boots on Cold floors Winter mornings Now can you Mr Bennett
Honestly Can you I say You Cannot You would Be Surprised How
Many are Wakeing up about Our Government. Don't you think that
it is High Time You cut Some of that Awful Expense out and let us
Live The Few Remaining Years in a little more Comfort
   You are in The Position too do So If You Want
   Sorry I have not time to make it Plainer And Trusting There will
soon Be a Big Difference   I am English came out 1910

Sincerely
(Mrs) Clara Leibert

[*Agnes C. Macphail was the first woman elected to the House of
Commons, MP for South-east Grey (Ont.) 1921-35, Grey-Bruce
1935-40. Variously a leading member of the Progressive party,
'Ginger Group,' CCF, and United Farmers of Ontario.]

489338-40

Montreal 23 Decembre 1933

Très Honorable Mr Bennett
Jose madressé a vous pour savoir si vous pourriez pas faire quelque
chosse pour nous autre   je suis mere de 14 enfants dont 12 sont
vivant et la plus vielle est agé de 15 ans seulement et la plus jeune a
seulement que 15 jour elle est né le 9 decembre 1933. J'espere
davoir droit a une petite prime comme etant mère d'une nombreusse
famille dans si peu de temps de ménage. Jai seulement que 33 ans et
mon mari 35 ans et sa fait 16 ans que nous sommes marié, si vous
aimé à avoir lage et le nom de mes enfants les voici

Violet né	3 Octobre 1918
André	28 Janvier 1920
Thérèse	28 Mars 1923
Patricia	21 Novembre 1924
Armande	25 Janvier 1926
Jeanne	30 Janvier 1927

Rita   15 Avril 1928
Jacques   30 Juin 1929
Claire   1 ier Novembre 1930
Denise   28 Octobre 1931
Henriette   15 Novembre 1932
Germaine   19 decembre 1933
    et 2 filles décéde
    une Patricia Jeanine né le 10 mai 1921
    et l'autre pas batisé
    moi la mère je suis né le 5 novembre 1900 mon mari né le 20
    Aout 1898
et marié le 10 septembre 1917
mon mari est un Soldat retour du front ils appartenait dans le 41 ier
Batt. son nom est Alp. Henri Lacasse et voila deja 2 ans que mon
mari ne travaile pas
    en esperent de recevoir une reponse au plus vite que possible

Mad. A.H. Lacasse

Merci

483392-4

Dec 30/33

BRIEF PRESENTED BY THE UNEMPLOYED OF EDMONTON
TO THE HON. R.B.BENNETT

Mr. R.B.Bennett
Prime Minister of Canada

For three long, weary years you, Mr. Bennett and your Conservative
Party have held undisputed and unmolested sway in Canada. You
and your coleagues were elected primarily because you gave the
people two great promises, (1) you would end unemployment, (2)
you would blast your way to foreign markets. As to the first of these

promises, you Mr. Bennett as the chief Economic Doctor, have
failed, miserable failed, not only to cure the dangerous disease, but
even to give it an unbiased diagnosis; and the only blasting that has
been apparent has been the inhuman wrecking of millions of once
happy homes. You have repeatedly reminded us of the sacredness of
our British Institutions. Mr. Bennett, is not the home an institution?
Then why do you callously stand by while it is being wantonly destroyed by the Molloch of Big business? We have this to say Mr.
Bennett. Even a yellow dog will resist, to the death, the ruthless
destruction of his most priceless possession.
Surely, in three years of full political power you could have found, if
you had tried, a better method of dealing with unemployment than
the Direct Relief System. In view of the fact that you have not we
hereby give you the only solution which is applicable in society as at
present constituted. Non-contributary Unemployment Insurance. It
must be non-contributary, otherwise the million and a half already
unemployed will receive no benefit. Pending the enactment of this
Bill, Relief allowances must be raised. Seeing that we are not allowed
to earn in wages sufficient to maintain us and our families, we
demand adequate relief. The perpetual cry of Mayor Knott, and
Premier Brownlee is "We can do nothing. We have no money". Without discussing the truthfulness of these statements, Mr. Bennett, we
know that the contribution from the Federal Treasury must be
doubled if it is designed to even remotely approach the need. The
Paris Cannaille stood outside the aristocratic gates and watched good
food which they required, being thrown to the dogs. Later, they got
something to eat. Mr. Bennett must history repeat itself? We have
not words in our vocabulary sufficiently strong to properly condemn
your method of dealing with unemployed single men. Those slave
camps are a blot on the record of any civilized country. That young
men, the very flower of the race, those who must make the next
generation are forced, by economic necessity, to enter those isolated
prisons, where there is neither proper physical food, nor mental
stimulation, cries to Heaven for correction. What are you trying to
do to our young men? Make a generation of physical wrecks and
mental dolts? Or perhaps they will be used for cannon fodder? The
militarization of those camps strongly points to this latter hy-
pothesis as being the correct one. The hypocrisy of sending a dele-
gation to Geneva, and at the same time placing the single men in

camps under the control of the Department of National Defence is too apparent to be overlooked. We shall resist to the bitter end the slaughtering of those boys and young men in an Imperialist war. We demand that they be taken out of those camps and be given an opportunity to earn a civilized living, at a civilized wage, and live a normal life by taking a wife and raising a family. We protest against the increased appropriations for the National Defence. These monies should never be spent for these purposes, but instead, used to supplement the contribution to relief. The battleships and bombing planes, and big guns will never be used if it is left to the people to declare war. In this connection why has Japan been allowed to buy tremendous quantities of junk iron from Canada? Is it possible we shall again see and feel this iron in the form of bullets? If such a thing should come to pass, who is the butcher, the man behind the gun or the man who supplied him with the ammunition. We want it clearly understood that we consider the workers of Japan, Germany, France, Russia or any other country as nothing more nor less than brother workers and we strongly protest against the despicable and abominable part Canada is playing in hastening us toward another great Imperialist conflagation, the horrors of which were only too well forcast by the last World War.

Mr. Bennett, there was never a more damnable insult heaped upon a working class of any country than when armoured tanks and other highly perfected instruments of slaughter were sent into Stratford, Ontario.* Are these the trying circumstances which will test the very best of our National fibre, which you mentioned upon your return from England? Why is it, that if our government is a Democratic institution, representing the whole people the armed forces of the nation is used to coerce the working class, who make up 95% of the population, and force them to submit to wage cuts and a general worsening of their living conditions? On the face of it, it appears that Big business, whose interest it is to force the working class into pauperism, is being protected and not we; that the minority is dictatorial machine [sic], which our Democratic government allows to use the military power of the nation against the majority. Not only in Stratford does this phenomena manifest itself, but throughout the country, whenever the workers use the only economic weapon they have, the strike, the R.C.M.P. are rushed to the spot and club the workers into submission. We submit Mr. Bennett that we are a peaceful people. If you will send work at a living wage to strikers instead of tanks and machine guns your economic troubles will be considerably lessened. We protest against this Fascist terrorism, and demand the rights of free speech and free assemble. We protest against the policy of deporting foreign born workers simply because they can find no buyer for their labor power. The solidarity of the British Commonwealth of Nations is widely publisized, yet, we find workers born in the British Isles are subject to deportation. When a young and great country like Canada with only Ten million population finds itself in the position where it must deport labor power there must be something wrong with its economic system. Those workers, came to Canada in good faith, after being led to believe that this country was the land of their dreams. They did not come in order to get on Canada's Unemployed list. After promising them a Heaven, and then give them Hell is not a safe policy. The slightly lesser evil of the relief lists is, we feel, the worst that these people should be subject.

To sum up, Mr. Bennett, we are absolutely fed up with being on relief. The terrible waste that is implied in a million and a half idle man power is a crime against the human race. There is so much work to do, and here are, unemployed. We don't know how the natural resources come to be where they are, but we do know, that neither you nor Big business created them. The material is here, land, lumber, iron, steel, etc. and so are we. If you can't supply the tokens of exchange that will bring us together, you had better resign and hand the country over to the workers. We may be ignorant uncouth men, belong to the lowest strata of a low society, but, and we don't boast, we will have enough sence to eat when there is food to eat, and work when there is work to be done and tools to work with.

[*In September 1933 troops were sent to Stratford, Ontario, at the request of the Ontario government, to keep order in an industrial dispute involving the furniture and meat-packing workers. The fully-armed contingent was equipped with four machine-gun carriers that were described in the press as tanks.]

490257-60

Toronto, Ont.
15th Jan. 1934.

Sir:—

I do wish you would put into operation some form of work as I do not think that the present form of Direct Relief is beneficial. Men are becoming discouraged and lazy! Why not help to keep their morale up? What is relief, anyhow, but charity?

I am not ungrateful for the help which I have had this past year, but I am so tired of this existance. I see no hope for the future. I had hopes of educating my sons to take their place in life and to be worthy citizens of the land of their birth, but I see nothing but poverty ahead of us. It is nearly four years since we have had any work on the building. There are eight children—all normal, healthy and bright. We have lost and sold all our material possessions and have come to live in the poorest part of the city and now we are facing the possibility of not being able to pay our rent. My husband is a first-class plastering contractor who worked on the ornamental work of the Leyland Stanford University, California and has always looked after his wife and family. We are Conservatives for generations past—landed gentry in Scotland—paupers in Canada.

I myself am a Proofreader and would be only too willing to work if I could get a position. Please give the matter of building your very earnest consideration during the forthcoming conference. You are a bachelor and cannot realize what it is to know you are responsible for the welfare and care of eight children who ought to have a much better heritage—in this land of vast resourses—than poverty. Surely something can be done.

I have written the Governor. General to ask for Deportation, as Mr. Trehern could get lots of work in England.

Trusting to hear from you, I remain,

Yours respectfully,
Coleen Trehern

484369-70

Winnipeg, Manitoba
January 26th-1934

Dear Sir: —

I have been unemployed for nearly four years. I am a Canadian
born subject and I am forced to beleive that this is very detre-
mental in many ways.

Recently there were several families whom were to be deported
who were on Relief. In any other country these families *would
have been deported* but our Government apparently wishes to continue to pay and pay for these families. Not only that but they even
go so far as to assist them in receiving work. Something that I have
almost forgotten what it is.

I have written to you several times before seeking your assistance
in *securing employment,* but have only been successfull in receiving a type of letter that firms use as a stock letter to be sent to
several hundreds of thousand seeking information. In other words
these letters were written by your secretaries and in a manner to
distinctly indicate that I was just another nuisance and at that time I
was only partially as desperate to secure employment as I am now.

I have read item upon item of what your going to do but up to
date it is still a myth in regard to action. If you are as ambitious
to assist your countrymen as you state at many times you could help
me and be assured that it truly would be appreciated.

I am an Electrical worker by trade and had worked for the
Manitoba Telephone System for some years. I am experienced in
many branches of this work as well as other lines.

I have had an application for employment with the Dominion
Telegraph Service for sometime. You could with your connections secure some employment in this branch if you wished to for
me.

I am married and have three children and it is because of them
that I am striving to secure employment.

I also have a Certificate of Seamanship which qualifies for a
Seaman.

I also have a Chauffeur's license and above all I have two hands
and a willing head to do some work and I am not particular what
the nature is.

We have been forced to exist on crusts four years too long. Have you tried it? It is very nourishing and very encouraging to tramp around in an endeavour to secure work. Some people like it but here's one that is disgusted to realize that because he is a Canadian by birth and has to stand for such Ballyhoo as is being shot around by our Government especially in upholding our laws regarding Immigration.

Let this same family go into the States and see where they stop at. *They would be deported* regardless. But they get the break here in Canada. There are possibly 500,000 Immigrants in Canada that are holding back the native of Canada from getting employment but a little thing like that does not both a man when he has a full stomach. Take for instance yourself you are well fed, financially in a position to live in a correct fashion, and all the other pleasures that you may desire. Just for a moment put yourself on the other side of the fence and figure it out why should I be of the attitude I am. Would you be? You would not be worthy of the position you now hold if you did not feel the same.

Arrange for a loan of $1500.00 from the Government for me and I'll take my family and leave the country of my birth because no matter how hard I try I cannot get work here.

According to routine this letter will not reach you personally but will be handled by some one of your clerks to answer that you are sorry that it is impossible for you to do anything and that you are sorry that I am in the position that I am and that you will forward my letter to the Mayor of the City of Winnipeg as all employment is handled by the Municipality.

I have mentioned previously in this letter that I would like to secure a loan. I have been employed in United States and am confident that I would be successful in securing employment there as I have certain experience in certain lines of work in which there is always a scarcity of workers.

Also another way of looking at it is that during the past four years I have been an expense of approximately $2400.00 to the Dominion of Canada and the prospects are that the expense will amount to considerably more than this before I die.

The $1500.00 mentioned could be repaid in a period of 5 years and it would be the means of my re-establishment.

At the same time bear in mind that you would be assisting 5 persons to get off the Releif. This is a point to be considered.

Why not discuss this plan with the various members of Parliament? But above all please take the matter up personally and let me know the results.

My own case of Releif has been discussed at many meetings of Relief authorities here and I am well known in person. I belong to no organization and have always tried to fight my own way.

With your assistance I can once more become a *respectable* law abiding citzen and if I am not successful in securing your help. Then what do you think I would do. Remember I am desperate.

As I wish this letter to be addressed to you personally I am addressing it as Personal which the nature of it is.

At present I am a Law Abiding Canadian born Citizen and trust that I shall be able to remain lawfully.

I am Sir,
Yours Very Truly,
Charles Grierson

P.S. This letter addressed to Hon. R.B.Bennett in person.

[See also letters from Grierson on pp. 22, 46, 151, 156, 161, 172.]

398060-4

Toronto
Jan 28. 1934

Dear Mr. Bennett.

Maybe you have never received a letter from any of the public about conditions. Us fellows down here are getting fed up with all your paper talk, what we want is action and pretty quick, we have been bluffed along by your big talk   Why dont you cut off about 2 or 3 thousand dollars from all theese big men and put men to work out of it what your doing is taking all you can get your hands on taxing us poor people so as you can make enough money to go to Florida for a vacation or England   You once made a speech about

you would have all the men back to work as soon as you got in that
was a lot of hooey   You can do what you like to me for writing
you this letter it is all true. What we need is a new Goverment all
through and us fellows down here are going to see we get it. I am
telling you this something is going to happen soon if things dont get
moving. Men want money how do they get it why steal it. Why?
because you fellows who have it all wont part with it there are more
men going to prison now than ever there was mostly the younger
generation whereas if they had an steady job with a pay envelope
comming every week there wouldn't be any. I myself has been out
of work for 2 years have no people am an emigrant have been over
here 10 years. Was brought out by Dr. Barnardo's Home* placed on
a farm for 150 dollars the first two years I was out there 5 years and
I ruined my spine I write and ake for help what do I get all they can
do is send me up North to a camp when I am not fit   I wont go.
you say how you worked your way up to where you are times where
different then than now. I am a single man age 21 years old. I write
the Buildings for work. I get two days after not working for two
years   Have been a Good Canadian citizen and when I write Mr.
Henery he always says he will (endever) to get me work that was last
April. I need clothes my teeth need fixing. I owe 200 dollars room
and board, how can I get out of debt on just two days $7.20. There
are men in the Buildings who shouldnt be working they are cripples
they should be pensioned off and us younger fellows given a chance.
Look at me I earned $15.00 a week as shipper & Receiver I saved
about $50.00 in the bank after paying out $8.00 a week room and
board & Laundry. I banked $5.00 a week, I get laid off I have to use
it all for my board & room and now I get deeper every day. All I
want is a steady job of some kind a good living wage and I'll be all
set. All I do is live in hopes I get the same old answer every place I
go (no help wanted). Surely you can get me in down at the Buildings
here   Pleas send me a signed letter from yourself saying I can start I
can do office work or even help in the shipping room he is helpless
he comes down like this   a man like him could use a good

strong young man in there at any wage. Please see if you can get me in.

A Carpenter

[*The Barnardo homes, founded in England by Dr Barnardo in 1870, placed British orphans on farms in the dominions where they worked as a form of indentured labour until reaching maturity.]

484409-12

Naseby, Manitoba
Jan 29, 1934

Premier Bennett
Parliament Building
Ottawa
Ontario
Canada

We you know we have nothing up here dryed out & eat out with grasshoppers   nothing to eat outside or in   horses no oats for years   asking help for both out side & in
    My children has not enough to eat. Please try & do some thing. We are in Claywater Municipality in Albert   along side of me they get lots of help, & everything just what they should get horses starving. farmer suffering to much in every way come & see for yourself you can't belive till you see, try & come

Mrs. G. T. McTavish

[Reply: $5.00.]

398987

Upsalquitch N.B.
Fev. 2 1934

To Hon. R.B.Benett
Prime Minister of Canada

Dear Sir as I'm a widow and with five children I have recourse to
you I try everything regarding the Parish relief and it is impossible
for me to live with what they gave me I suffer with hunger cold etc.
listen to this I have a great confidence to you after God you are the
only man who can help me, in the month of January they gave me
$3.00 to live 6 persons I don't know how I could give my children
three meals a day with so Small quantity. I tell you we are suffering
and a great many in Upsalquitch I think I have more right than anybody else to complain as I am a widow and I have an awful trouble
for the wood.

My husband is dead a year ago he took is death in the Dalhousie
Jail or Prison they put him in for an account of $29. and he took
a lung inflamation he ask for the doctor and they told him it was not
an hospital the Prison was wet on account of having washed it and
he slept in that state I went to a lawyer he told me if I had the
money I will have my right but I was too poor to go with that in a
process I wrote to the Provincial Government without any Success I
hope that you will understand me and help me I don't think its a
reason to let your voters die because they are poor a great many are
Intelligent people and dies in distress.
Dear Hon. Sir a great many people here understand your Wisdom I
am one who respect you and hope in you remain yours in note am in
confidence

Mrs. Daria Collinet
Widow

481790-3

Beeton Station, Quebec
9 Fevrier 1934

Honorable R.B. Bennett
Ottawa

Cher Monsieur
    Veuillez bien me pardonner si je me permets de vous demander
du secours. Comme je ne puis rien obtenir du conseil après plu-
sieurs demandes j'ai pensé de m'adresser à vous, peut-être que vous
ne me refuserai pas. J'ai travaillé pour vous il y a quelques années et
je vais travailler encore à l'avenir   Je suis malade depuis 5 ans, il y a
4 ans j'ai passé 6 mois à l'hôpital et depuis ce temps j'ai toujours fait
ce que j'ai pu pour donner le nécessaire à ma famille   aujourd'hui je
ne plus rien faire du tout. Il faudrait que je retournerais à l'hôpital
sans faute, le medecin me dit que je ne peut pas vivre bien des années
sans soins. J'ai 6 enfants en bas âge, je suis âgé de 42 ans je n'ai pas
d'argent, nous avons plus de nourriture, on est sans vètements tout
ce qu'on est—pensez-y mon cher M. R.B. Bennett un hiver froid
comme on a. Les enfants se lamentent—de la faim et du froid   je
suis dans l'impossibilité de leur fournir le besoin qu'il demande
avec franchise c'est bien triste—
    J'espère que ma lettre sera prise en considération et recevoir une
réponse sous-peu
    Veuillez me croir M. R.B.Bennett, Je demeure

Votre tout devoué
Arsene Gaudet

483363-5

Lambert, Sask.
Feb. 23 1934

Honorable R.B.Bennett
Winnipeg Man.

Your Honor:—
   I am writing you regarding Relief   Will you please tell me if we
can get Steady relief & how much we should be allowed per week we
have three children 2 of School age, one boy is going to School
Some day's he cant go to school as we have no food in the house & I
wont let him go those day's. He has one Suit of under wear one pair
overalls one pair sock's one pair moccasin rubbers & that all the
clothes he has, not even a top shirt or a pair of trousers & the girl she
cant go to school as she hasent proper clothing to go with & the
little boy five years of age is in bad need of clothing Mr. Warden
hasent had a Job sence the Seven Sisters poer house construction job
was completed & I'll tell you weve had a hard struggle ever Since. we
came to Lambert we came here on the intentions of taking up a
home stead & we couldnt locate any land suitable & the water here
is rank. everytime I go up to ask the Mayor here in lambert for any
asistances he always Says he cant help us as the town is broke & he
Say's they cant get any asistance from the Government he Says he
was talking to Hodgson & Hodgson only laughed at him Hodgson
even told me that he doesnt think lambert needs any asistance as
they have such good crop's here I told him we cant eat the crop's as
they are not our's Mr Warden was out thrashing last fall & he made
Nine Dollars the only work the town of Lambert has for to be done
this winter is sawing wood for the Skating rink by Buck Saw at the
rate of 75¢ per cord its cord wood & you have to cut two cuts   So a
man cant make a living at that for his family nor he cant feed his self
good enough to give him strength to be able to saw the wood its Just
terrible the way the Mayor uses the unemployed here we are living in
a shack two rooms a bed room Just enough room for two beds & the
house is cold theres two inches of Ice freezes on the water in the
house cold nights we are shivering in bed at night we have no mat-
resses on our beds. only gunny Sacks & not enough blankets on our
beds. Mr. Warden has no under wear no top shirt no Socks only rags
on his feet no trousers only overauls. & they are done for, boots are

near don my Self I have no house dresses & no wash tub & when I
tell Mayor Veal those thing's he says why dont you go back to
Manitoba where you came from its a nice thing for a old country
english man to tell a Canadian in its own country Eh. he cant get
away from old england way's he Says if we had Some friends to stay
with hed pay our way back to Winnipeg & I tell him if we could get
a home stead & the farm loan we would be all right then but what
can we do for food & clothing till such a time to come there are
times we live on potatoes for days. at a time & its lasting So long I
dont see how much longer it can last all I have in the house now is
potatoes & there are good meny people the same in this town   I am
five months pregnant & I havent even felt life yet to my baby & its I
feel quite sure for the lack of food. there has been babys died in this
town from neglect those english men when they get any athority of
any kind in Canada they think they can make their own law's   Veal
Say's relief aint compulsery. now your honor, I Sincerely believe
you will help us as I know you did the country heaps of good when
you deported those emigrants for they are the cause of the crime
that has been comitted why do we want foreigners here & Send our
Canadians to be Slaughtered in War for them to live on the fat of the
land during the War & after if them people wants war let them fight
it we didnt start it   I know you Sure have done good although I
hear people Saying this and that I dont believe it for I have a mind
of my own. I must close hoping to get a reply at your earliest date
Your's truly

Mrs C.L.Warden

PS/Your Honor.
    I have been having a few words in conversations with a few
Inglish people. they say Canada has to go to War if Ingland call's
her & I Said she didnt for Canada owes nothing to Ingland & they
Said I was crazy because Canada belonged to england I sure would
like to know if I were right or they inglishmen were right
    the two oldest children & I are Suffering from abscess teeth can
we get them out & have the Town pay for the Dental Bill Mr.
Warden had three abscess teeth pulled this winter & charged it up to
the town with an order from the Mayor. & we never hear the end of
it every time we go to ask for food he throws that up to Such a

expence for having teeth out & the children & I have to have our bad
teeth out will you kindly give me advice on this.

489565-74

Calgary, Alta

Mr Bennet
No doubt you and your Cabinet have heard that the Voice of Many
Many People are against you   So you will need to listen with your
Ear to the ground
from you ever true friend

Robert T. Fairley

Debden, Sask.
March 3rd 1934

Hon. Mr. R.B.Bennet
Ottawa, Canada

Dear Sir—I am writing to see if you could not give me a little help. I
hear you are going to destroy some thousands of tons of wheat to
get rid of it; while my family & stock are starving to death. There is
lots of wheat and other things here but I have no money to buy
them with. I have been farming in Central Sask. since 1909 until a yr
ago when I was forced off my farm. So last yr. I could not get a
place for to farm so could only get what I could by working out on
farms. Which was not near enough to keep my family in food. In the
fall I moved to the North hoping to be able to keep my stock alive
and to be able to get a homestead. I had applied to have my stock
sent to Spiritwood but by some mistake somewhere I was sent to
Debden instead so then I had neither buildings or feed in reach and

dead broke in bitter cold weather. So could not buy feed or take a
homestead either. As the relief officer for this part was in town here
at the time I asked him for relief & for feed. I could not get any feed
whatever out of him until my four horses and seven head of cattle
(my two best cows included) 16 pigs (some of them weighed over
100 lbs) and most of my poultry had actually starved to death. All
that was necessary was an order to get some feed from the relief
officer, but though I asked him several times & did not get any until
that many were dead. Since then I have had orders amounting to
1500 (fifteen hundred) oat sheaves but nothing to feed a pig or
chicken. If I had been given sufficient feed in the first place my
stock would be alive and most of those hogs would now be ready for
market. We would then have some meat for our table and the rest
would have repaid the relief I needed and most likely would have
left something to take me off the relief list for a time at least. Now
we cannot farm the land I had rented because I haven't a horse left
to farm with. We kept off relief as long as we had a cent to buy food
or a rag of clothes that would hang together. To date we have had
$45.35 for food to feed ten of us from Dec. 1st on until now, and I
did relief bridge work to about that amount and was quite willing to
do as much more as I would get the chance to do. But when I asked
for a greater food allowance I was told that many were doing with
much less as well as one insult upon another added thereto by the
local relief officer. Yet I know several families right around here
getting more relief according to the size of family and do not need
relief at all but still they get it. I have 8 children ranging from 4½
yrs. to 14½ yrs. yet all we have had in the house for over a week has
been dry bread and black tea and believe me Mr. Bennet it isn't very
nice to listen hour after hr to young children pleading for a little
butter or why can't we have some potatoes or meat or eggs. But how
can I get it on what I have been getting when it takes most of it for
flour alone. Because we were not sent where we asked to be sent to
we have to live ten of us in cold one roomed shack instead of having
a comfortable house to live in. We haven't a mattress or even a tick
just simply have to sleep on a bit of straw and nearly every night we
have to almost freeze because we haven't bed clothes. I did not ask
relief to supply these but I did ask for pants, overalls and footwear
for the children about two months ago, but to date we have had
$15.95 of clothing (some of this had to be returned as it did not fit)

and some of the children are all this time running barefooted & not
one of them has had either a pr. of pants or overalls to cover their
nakedness. Neither can they go to school because they have no
clothes and also because the local school board demand a tuition fee
of $30 because we are not taxpayers as yet in this school and that
after paying school taxes in this province for nearly 25 years. One
result now is that the whole family have some kind of rash and running sores & I cannot take them to a Dr. as I have not the price to
pay the Dr. or to buy the things that he would order. Also my wife
has become badly ruptured and I can not have anything done about
it for the same reason. I was born with one leg shorter than the other
and am physically not a strong man but I have always done all I've
been able to do and a lot more than many more able than I am and
I am not in the habit of wasting any time or money on drinking,
gambling or anything of the sort yet we have to sit here and see not
only our stock starve but see my wife & children starve as well, and
do the same myself. So for God's sake give us an order to get a few
bus. of wheat to help us live and to raise a few chickens and pigs to
eat at least and if we ever make enough to do it with I'll return it
with interest too.

Yours in need
P.R. Mulligan

489599-604

(Translation)
Nagawa, Sask.
March 8-34

To our National Leader,
Prime Minister R.B.Bennett,
Ottawa, Ont.

I have a great thing to ask of you. I need help, for I am in want. I am
writing in German because I cannot write English. I am a German-

Canadian. I have been sick for four years and cannot earn anything
at all. I have been living for four years with my parents. They have
helped me until now with food and clothing. But they had no crop
last year and cannot support me any longer because they can hardly
get along themselves. So now I am in need. I have no clothes, neither
underclothes nor outer clothes, and cannot let people see me. So
please give me some money so that I can buy clothes. Help me this
once, for when my parents get a crop again they will be glad to give
me food and clothing again. I trust that our national leader will not
overlook one of his people who is in trouble.

With best regards, I am
Yours truly,
Gerhard Schmidt

489620

Livernois N.B.
March 9-1934

To R.B.Benett

Dear Sir
I am very badly in kneed of help as I am not getting enough relief to
support my family there are 8 in family and I am only getting relief
for 6. two bags of flour a month and I have not got any potatioes
nor has not had all winter and I looked for potatioes on the relief
and they would not give me none I have no cow and they would not
give me any milk   I have been without milk up until last months
relief I got 2 cans for the first I do not get any butter I kneed it very
much as my wife is sick and the doctor ordered her good strengthen-
ing food   In fact we are practully starving as we dont get enough to
support us and my family has been starving and freezing all winter as
the relief commissioner will not give them any clothes what relief we
get only does us ten days as our living is all bread and no potatioes
this is a list of what we get a month

2 bags flour	2 lbs tea	10 lbs rolled oats
2 gals molasses	10 lbs sugar	4 lbs lard
10 lbs beans	4 lbs soap	2 small bags salt
10 lbs pork	2 gals oil	

this is all we get, and we are out of food half of the time   I will
have to get more help and potatioues as I cannot make two bags of
flour do me a month with out potatioes   I will have to get more
help and I have had to hall my relief a mile on a hand sled from
Chartwell as I have no horse as the Storekeepers at Livernois would
not fill my orders and had to hall it with nothing to eat, and had to
break the road all the way, as we have no road comissioner and you
know how the snow was this winter. there are people with 3 and 4
of a family getting more than I am getting and getting potatioes and
milk and butter and some got clothes now kindly tend to this at
once as my children are naked and starving

Yours Respectfully
Mr Arthur M. Sullivan

481822-6

Marystown Harbour. N.S.
April 2nd, 1934

Dear Sir—
    I am writing you a few lines to see if you would please tell me
how much relief a family can get to live on as I am a poor man
and have never had any work to earn a cent since last October and
have a big family to feed and my wife has been sick for over a year
and no way this winter to get medicine for her and we only have the
shell of a house to live in so you see we are pretty poor off and I
went to the relief fellows here and all they would give me was 9
dollars and I have to buy two bags of flour out of that and flour here
is $6 dollars and 40 cents for two bags and we have neither fish nore
meat of any kind and no potatoes so now you know what kind of a
living we get out of that 9 dollars a month it is terrible how they

treat poor people here in New Harbour so kindly answer right away
and tell me what you think about it if we had the money we would
send it to you to pay for answering this letter but please answer right
away and oblige yours truly

Mr. Jack. B. Stopes

Mr. R.B.Bennett
Otawa   Quebec   Canada
please answer by return mail

481521-2

Hamilton, Ontario
April 6, 1934

To His Excellency The Rt. Hon. R.B.Bennett,
Parliament Buildings,
Ottawa, Ontario.
Att: Mr. Bennett.

Dear Sir:
    I am writing you as a last resource to see if I cannot, through
your aid, obtain a position and at last, after a period of more than
two years, support myself and enjoy again a little independence.
    The fact is: this day I am faced with starvation and I see no pos-
sible means of counteracting or even averting it temporarily!
    If you require references of character or ability I would suggest
that you write to T.M. Sanderson of Essex, Ontario. I worked as
Stenographer and Bookkeeper with him for over three years in the
office of the Sanderson-Marwick Co., Ltd., in Essex. I feel certain
that you have made his acquaintance for he was President of the
Conservative Association at the time of the Banquet held in your
worshipful honour a few years ago.
    I have received a high-school and Business-college education and I
have had experience as a Librarian. My business career has been

limited to Insurance, Hosiery, and Public Stenography, each time in the capacity of Bookkeeper and Stenographer—briefly, General Office work.

My father is a farmer at Pilot Mound, Manitoba and during the past years his income has been nil, so I cannot get any assistance from him. In fact, until I joined the list of unemployed I had been lending the folks at home my aid. To save my Mother from worry I have continually assured her that I am working and till the end I will save her from distress by sticking to this story.

When the Sanderson-Marwick Co., Ltd., went out of business I had saved a little money and there being no work there for me I came to Hamilton. Since then I have applied for every position that I heard about but there were always so many girls who applied that it was impossible to get work. So time went on and my clothing became very shabby. I was afraid to spend the little I had to re-plenish my wardrobe. Always the fear was before me that I would fail to get the position and then I would be without food and a roof over my head in a short time. Many prospective employers just glanced at my attire and shook their heads and more times than I care to mention I was turned away without a trial. I began to cut down on my food and I obtained a poor, but respectable, room at $1 per week.

First I ate three very light meals a day; then two and then one. During the past two weeks I have eaten only toast and drunk a cup of tea every other day. In the past fortnight I have lost 20 pounds and the result of this deprivation is that I am so very nervous that I could never stand a test along with one, two and three hundred girls. Through this very nervousness I was ruled out of a class yesterday. Today I went to an office for an examination and the examiner just looked me over and said; "I am afraid Miss, you are so awfully shabby I could never have you in my office."

I was so worried and disappointed and frightened that I replied somewhat angrily:

"Do you think clothes can be picked up in the streets?"

"Well," he replied with aggravating insolence, "lots of girls find them there these days."

Mr. Bennett, that almost broke my heart. Above everything else I have been very particular about my friends and since moving here I have never gone out in the evening. I know no one here personally and the loneliness is hard to bear, but oh, sir, the thought of starvation is driving me mad! I have endeavoured to be good and to do what is right and I am confident I have succeeded in that score but I can name more than ten girls here in Hamilton who I am sure are not doing right and yet they have nice clothes and positions. That is what seems so unfair. They never think of God nor do they pray and yet they seem so happy and have so many things I would like, while I, who pray every night and morning have nothing!

Day after day I pass a delicatessen and the food in the window looks oh, so good! So tempting and I'm so hungry!

Yes I am very hungry and the stamp which carries this letter to you will represent the last three cents I have in the world, yet before I will stoop to dishonour my family, my character or my God I will drown myself in the Lake. However, I do not hint that I have the slightest intention of doing this for I am confident that you will either be able to help me find employment or God will come to my aid.

But in the meantime my clothing is getting shabbier and I am faced with the prospect of wearing the same heavy winter dress, that has covered me all winter, during the coming summer.

Oh please sir, can you do something for me? Can you get me a job anywhere in the Dominion of Canada. I have not had to go on relief during this depression but I cannot get relief even here. Moreover it is a job I want and as long as I get enough to live I shall be happy again.

I have tried to get work at anything and everything from housework up but I have been unsuccessful and now I am going to starve and in debt to my landlady. I wouldn't mind if I could just lay down and die but to starve, oh its terrible to think about.

Mr. Bennett, even if you can do nothing for me I want to thank you for your kindness in reading this letter and if I were jobless and semi-hungry for a life-time I would still be a Conservative to the last, and fight for that Government.

Thanking you again for your very kind attention, I am,

Your humble servant,
(Miss) Elizabeth McCrae

P.S. I have tried my hand at writing stories for the Canadian Home

Journal and MacLean's Magazine but they reject them saying that
my work is of too high and deep a quality for their paper. Could you
tell me of some magazine which I might submit them to and would
you lend your influence in helping me sell them? E.M.

395626-31

Roberval   7 Avril   1934

Launorable Mrs Bennette
Premier Ministe

Monsieur
    Je suis un pauvre cultivateur qui à passè l'hiver malade, et une
grosse famille et nayant rien à manger et rien à semer ma terre. je
dèmanderai donc de me donner du secour avec la grasse de Dieu ou
bien je vais mourir de fin. Veillez me croire

Votre tout devouè
Joseph Labrichière
Cultivateur

483523

Private
21/4/34
Montreal

Primeminister
Ottawa Ont

Dear Sir:—

Scores are each day being put on the St. in this city with no place
to go & you & your party blowing in millions on vanity: $1,000.00
per month on a dead head C.N.R.

Yet Gods creatures born in his own Image have not a place to
lay their heads: my own turn to go on the street falls on the 25th
inst.

I do not care so much for my-self its my good wife who comes
from a highly respectable family in Wales & my-self the son of a
respected Elder of one of the oldest Protestant Churches in N.S. I
am pleased to know that my Parents are not alive to know of the
cruel times in wich we live: is it any wonder that People are losing
faith in God & man: its a shame & a disgrace the way unemployed
have been treated in this city for the past 4 months You & your
Dept. of Labour are fully aware of the conditions that exist in the
city of Montreal

But what do you care for the poor man on the St.

Here is what your Finance Minister States in a letter to me dated
Feb 14-34 you, referring to my-self, apparently are under the im-
pression that because you served overseas you & your family should
be clothed & fed for the rest of your days. I know this man Rhodes.
When he was running on the streets of Amherst & Halifax in short
pants, & I think I am safe in saying I have done more real hard work
in one month than he has in all his life: & I am expecting no government to keep me & my family the rest of my days, & the statement
made by your Finance Minister is the kind of a statement that could
be expected from a rotter like Rhodes. I intend to hold this letter, it
will make splendid reading, Especially for the returned men of
Canada. You and your government can not plead ignorance to the
facts as they exist today, and you & your party will have to give an

answer to the question what are you doing for the unemployed.

Yours Etc.
Alexander McMorris

the Park bench Poet

483569-71

Port Cobourg Ont.
May 9th 1934

Dear Mr. Benet I cant spel very good to right I think my women is
coming to see me this summer from Detroit Mish. I didn't see her for
4 years and I have no close have you some old close you could send
me and I could meat my wife and I will do a good tarn for you yours
truly

Mickey Ratelle
Write soon

394709

Montréal, 24 juillet 1934

Très Honorable Mr. Bennett.
Premier Ministre

   Je viens m'addresser a vous pour vous demander si pourriez faire
quelque chose pour nous, voici notre cas, mon mari est sans ouvrage
depuis près de 2 ans ½, je suis une femme malade, je me fais soigner
à l'hopital Notre-Dame et à l'Institut Bruchési, j'ai maigris—de 40
livres   je pèse à peine 100 livres je perd beaucoup de forces, il me

faudrait du repos et une bonne nourriture, nous sommes sur le
secours directs mais nous en avons pas assez   il faut que je boive 1
pinte de lait par jour je n'en ai pas, c'est juste d'en avoir pour le
bèbé, je suis obligée de subir une operation je ne suis pas assez forte,
mais je ne peux pas renforcir n'ayant pas assez de manger pour
manger à ma faim, je suis bien découragée je ne sais plus quoi faire,
je perds des forces tous les jours, je me suis adressée à la Commission
du chômage pour avoir plus, et à la Saint-Vincent Paul, ils ne peuvent rien faire, alors nous avons personne pour nous venir en aide,
nous en avons trés grand besoin, faites quelque chose pour nous
autre   si vous pouviez avoir de l'ouvrage pour mon mari je vous
serait trés reconnaissante   si vous n'avez pas d'ouvrage, seriez vous
assez bon de nous faire parvenir 1 pinte de lait à tous les jours et un
peu de manger tous les semaines, car rendu au samedi nous n'avons
plus rien à manger   il nous reste que du pain et du beurre pour 3
jours je ne sais ce que nous allons devenir, car je suis malade et ne
pas avoir seulement assez de manger pour se nourrir.

J'en connais qui sont sur le secour direct et ils trouve le moyen de
boire leur argent tandis que nous nous privons du nécessaire   nous
n'avons plus rien à se mettre sur le dos   pas de souliers à se mettre
dans les pieds   mes enfants ont rien à porter. Je ne comprends pas
comment cela se fait-il une grande ville comme Montréal   quand on
s'adresse aux places pour nous aider, ils nous font marcher d'une
place à l'autre et à la fin personne ne peut rien faire.

Je suis rendu au bout, depuis 2 ans ½ ça fait 12 fois que nous
dèménageons c'est ces troubles qui me ruinent

Je vous demande, Monsieur l'Honorable Bennett de ne pas laisser
ma lettre sans réponse nous en avons trop besoin, et je sais que
votre bon coeur et votre bonté comprendra notre misère et fera
quelque chose pour la soulager   le Bon Dieu vous le rendra

Madame Albert Barton

483626-9

Personal
Calgary July 26-34

R.B.Bennett Esq
Prime Minister

Sir, As I have seen it in the press on different occasions that Ottawa imagines that there are those in Calgary getting Relief that are not entitled to it, I might say there a lot of people in Calgary are of the same opinion.

Although the Mayor & Mr. G. Thompson the Civic Relief Manager have both told me that if at any time I was suspicious of any one to inform them. I have mentioned the names of five different ones but they refuse to me the information asked for. They both have told me recently they haven't the time to talk with me.

I have been trying now for over a year to find out why a man on Relief was getting Relief for 2 children when I was informed he had only one of his own. They, the Mayor & Thompson, admit he was getting Relief for 2. But will not tell me if it was his own.

Another man (that came under my personal observation) was given $9.20 more than he ever expected to get after him telling them he could do without it as his wife was working part of the time. I saw the order. This man declared he was told to call agin in two weeks time and he would be given another order. He told me himself he could get along without it. A Third man admits that he has some C.P.R. Shares which as you know have been quoted at $16.00 or $17.00. In fact he admitted to the City Investigator he had sold some in the month of February.

My neighbor where this man roomed informed me besides having the C.P.R. Shares. Last winter purchased for cash a Divanette, 8 piece Dining room Suite, a Kitchen Cupboard, and a Stove, The stove costing $24.00. My neighbor said the man should be exposed. But as he had already reported some to the Civic Authorities & they hadn't taken any notice of it. It seemed useless to report. Hence my reason for reporting it & yet I presume this man took his oath month after month that he was absolutely destitute. The Fourth that came under my personal notice was a man that was earning some $5. or $6. per month as light Janitor duties. I have asked on different occasions if he reported those earnings. But up to the

present have been refused the information from both the Mayor &
Mr. Thompson. The provincial Investigator, Mr. Morrison (I believe
that is his name) knows about these cases. This man according to his
own word sold a car in September. They refuse to tell me if he
reported this Transaction.

Another that came under my personal notice was a man on
Relief that ran a car in 1933 & the latter of February took out a
1934 Car License for a large Nash Sedan. I received the information
direct from Mr. Sheritt the Manager of the Provincial License Office.
And at the same time he was lacking some $30.00 on Rent owing to
me.

The next man I was informed was getting Relief & yet at the
same time had a seat on the Exchange here. That was worth about
$1400.00 plus other valuables. According to my Information.

I am not saying that those on Relief are getting too much. Not by
any means But still I do not consider they should be allowed to get
away with anything shady.

I wrote Premier Reid a day or two ago. But as he had just left for
his Holiday. When I thought he would likely be at Ottawa on the
30th. I presume the Hon Mr. Hoadley would not have seen my communication before leaving for Ottawa. I might say that I am a
pioneer here in the West. Having come this side of Winnipeg in 97.
Have brought Hundreds of acres of the prairie under cultivation.
Some with oxen & some with horses. Now in my 69th year. Am
not earning as much as those that are getting through Relief. In fact
I am not getting a cent for what I am doing. I estimate I do $500.00
worth of work a year at only one half as much per hour as those that
are on Relief. And the Farm that is now Rented on shares runs in
debt.

Trusting Honourable Sir you will pardon me for taking the liberty
of writing you. Can give the names of these men.

Yours Truly
Fred Tinsley

[Reply]

Ottawa, August 1, 1934.

Dear Mr. Tinsley:
    I have before me for acknowledgment your letter of the 26th of
July, directed to the Prime Minister.
    I note you state that cases have come under your personal obser-
vation where the recipients of relief are in possession of stocks or
bonds, or are otherwise ineligible for the relief they are receiving. If
you will send me the names of these people, together with their
addresses, I will bring the matter to the attention of the City authorities in order that their claim for relief may be investigated.

Yours faithfully,
Secretary.

491161-5

James Stn, Ont
Sept. 11th/34

Dear.
Rt Honorable R.B.Bennett. Just a line to ask you if you can give me
clothes for the children to go to school. I would like if I could get
clothes for all my children as I have 10 childrens and If I could get
some lumber from the Government to build a house as I am living
about 5 miles back in the bush and I would like to build a house
near the school. There is no way to make money as they wont take
him on the road. If you can't give me lumber to build a house would
you pay the rent if I moved into town.
    Let me know what you can do for me by return of mail

From Mrs Muriel Balle

394737

Montreal 10-22-34

To his Excellency: The Premier

Dear Sir.
   Well I just left the releif office where I saw a Chinaman that
couldnt read or write english or french apply for releif, that been in
the Country since 1928. on previous occasion I saw Chines, Negros,
and Greeks get releif checks, on July 2nd 1934 I applied for releif,
but I havent realized any yet; altho my Grandfather and Grandmother
settled here around 1835 my Father Mother and myself were born
here, and I am destitute. Feed, Clothe and House the foreign, while
the natives starve and freeze is the slogan of our local politicians.

Robert Jackson

483681

Hamilton, Ont.
Oct. 24th 1934

The Rt.Hon. R.B.Bennett,
Prime Minister of Canada
Parliament Buildings
Ottawa, Canada

Dear Sir,
   In the midst of all your duties I am taking the privilege of
addressing you in regard to a matter that has been on my mind for
several years. I have heard department store girls complain in my
hearing that no one cares for them. I have heard girls talking as they
walked along the streets, as recently as this morning, "you have to
work there from 7 A.M. 5 P.M. for $7.00 or 8.00 a week." Now
my thought has not been so much for the girl with a job for I'm sure
the Hon. Mr Stevens and yourself will adjust working conditions
before the enquiry* is finished. But my thought is *"What are we*

doing in the way of relief for the single girl without a job?" There
are young women who have no home being without support of
mother, father, brother, or husband. Are we going to stand aside and
see prostitutes made of our Canadian women. I was born in Winnipeg over 40 years ago, and ever since I was a boy it has been a standing joke among boys and men of Canada, that our working girls were
expected to make something on the side immorally, to help support
them. We ought to clean up our own house before throwing stones
at our neighbors, anyway the Scripture says "Let him who is without sin cast the first stone" also "Love worketh no ill to his neighbor". We want Canada to be an unstanding example to the rest of
the world in following after Peace and in other Christian teachings.

I'm a returned soldier and an ordained Christian minister and I
believe you are a man of action so I'm writing direct to you. We have
the Lions Club and other places for single men & married men to get
relief but I do not know of municipalities giving meals or rooms to
destitute women. I may be misinformed, however you will know the
conditions or make it your business to find out.

I am, your obedient servant,

F.T.McDougall

P.S. If the Premiers of the Provinces have another meeting, this matter could be brought to their attention successfully.

[*The Select Committee on Price Spreads and Mass Buying was
established in February 1934 under the chairmanship of H.H.
Stevens, minister of trade and commerce; it was reappointed in July
1934 as the Royal Commission on Price Spreads and Mass Buying.
See introduction.]

486569-70

Compton P. Que.

Hon Mr R.B.Bennett
Chambre de Commues
Ottawa

Dear Hon. Sir,

No doubt you recives numorus letters like this one which I am
sending you, but I would so much want my letter to impress you so
that you would favor us with your great kindness. We are poor
people living on a farm far out in the country and we have had more
than our share of bad luck. We lost some live stock last winter and
now we are more at loss than ever how to make both ends meet, as
my husband has just had 2 fingers cut off from his left hand and has
been under the doctor's care for the past 4 weeks. The doctor says
that he will not be able to work for 2 or 3 months more which you
see leaves us very much at loss how to get food & clothing. We have
some debts to pay also the taxes on our farm and a payment due
(past) and the M.D. Bills already amount to $50.00. Now the ques-
tion is Could you find us some way with which to get some money
to pay the Dr. at least a bit as he wishes to be paid. We are a family
of 6. 4 young children & ourselves and we would not want to lost
our farm as it is our only means of a living. Could you suggest us
some way to pull through?

As for me (Mrs Lejoi) I am sending you a hooked rug. Perhaps
Mrs Bennett* would like it and send us some worn clothing in return
mens suits, shoes Womans wear & children's wear etc. Anything &
Everything would be greatly appreciated as what we cannot wear as
it is we make over for the children. We do not mind wearing patches
as we are far out in the country & we wear what we can get. Or if
you care to keep the rug won't you please send us some little favor it
would mean so much to us with wich to buy food with. I am sure
you must have some shoes clothing etc which you could send in
return for the rug. Won't you please try & help us with your great
kindness. Your answer means so much to us. It does not need much
to put a silver linning into our dark clouds. If you do not care to
keep the rug won't you please try & dispose of it amongst your
friends or please return it to us as soon as possible. Havent you some
friends who would care for some rugs and send clothing etc in

return. I have some very pretty ones.

May we look forward to your great kindness as soon as possible.

With the Best of Wishes for your Good Health and continued Success.

Gratefully Yours.
Mr & Mrs Felix Lejoi

Answer Soon please

[*R. B. Bennett was a bachelor.]

[Reply: $5.00.]

398620-3

B.C.   Dec. 1934.

Canadian Govt. at Ottawa, Canada

Well Mr. R.B.Bennet, arnt you a *man* or are you? to be the cause of all this starvation and privation. You call us derelicts, then if *we* are derelicts *what else are you* but one too. only *a darn sight worse.* You said if you was elected, you would give us all work and wages, well you have been in the Prime Ministers shoes, now, for 4 years. and we are *still looking for work and wages.* You took all our jobs away from us. We can't earn any money. You say a releif camp is good enough for us, then *its too good* for *you* Mr Bennet, you are on releif your own self. You put away your big govt salary, then ask the gov't. to pay for your big *feasts,* while *we* poor fellows starve. While *you* jazz around the hotel girls. You think people don't know any-thing well, even if we are *"derelicts" "as you called us",* and which we consider you as the leader of the derelicts Band you have fooled us a lot, in the last four years. We have lived on your hot air, so you may know you had to expell a *lot* But you can't fool *all* of us, *all* the time.

You are nothing short of a murderer when you hired that man by name of Smith to shoot Tim Buck in the jail.* Well now Mr. Bennet, I hope this sinks clear down to your toes, and gives you swelled feet, instead of a swelled head. You have had a swelled head ever since you had the "Eddy" Match Co. signed to you by Mrs. Eddy,† don't think people don't know anything.

P.S. this will take my last 3 cents, but we hope it goes to the bottom of *you,* and that you will hand us out *both work* and *living wages.* You have caused *lots* of people to kill their families and themselves rather than to slowly starve to death, or freeze to death. Try it you prime minister, just try it.

Now you are trying to get war going to make yourself richer. Well R.B.Bennet, I hope you get your share of the bullets.

We are going to give you a chance, (which you don't deserve.) either you will stop this war, now, and give us fellows work and living wages enough to stop such starving, and freezing, because we *can't* buy any clothes, the doukabours are jailed because they wont wear any clothing while *we* are jailed trying to get clothing to wear. You say we live too extravagance, then you shall be able to hand out $5.00 to anyone and everyone, then we wont live so extravagant. You have heaps of money laid away. Well, it wont do you a bit of good if we have another war.

We are giving you this chance   We say again you do not deserve it at all. If we dont get work or wages, and "living wages" to, we are going to tell the Canadian government they have a "murderer", in the house at Ottawa. You said a rich uncle left you your wealth, bah. We know better. We are not trying to scare you, but we are tired, of relief camps and going hungry and cold. no homes, or any thing else.

[*Five shots were fired into the cell of Tim Buck, leader of the Communist Party of Canada, by prison guards during rioting at Kingston Penitentiary in October 1932.]

[†Bennett inherited stock in the Eddy Match Company valued at approximately $400,000 from Jennie Shirreff Eddy, a close friend

from childhood, in 1921. In 1926 he inherited shares worth about
$1,500,000 from her brother, Joseph Thompson Shirreff.]

492713-6

Crest Willow Alberta
Dec 11. 1934

To Right H.R.B.Bennett.

Your Honour
      I had my crop completely hailed out, I applied to the Munici-
pality for relief. I am on the sick list, & the Counciler got a certificate from the Docter that I was not to do any work I have a bad
alcerated stomach, so that I could not go on the road to work. The
Counciler told me I would get $6.00 per month for myself and
$8.00 for my Wife & daughter between them. They held me up for
two months longer then all the rest, then a week ago sent us $8.00
order for groacery. I am the only one here treated like this. If it had
not been for our Storekeeper we would have starved I have been
here nearly 22 years and have never asked for anything before. If I
was a *foreinger* or a *red* I would get the best of treatment, has it
happens I am a *Loyal Englishman* There is a lot of unjust work going
on with this releif. There is lot getting it that should not get it. An
Englishman could die here nobody trouble's about him.
      Will you please give this your consideration has we need fair play
at once. I had to return the Docters medicine that he sent through
the mail, Has I had not the money to pay for it.

Yours faithfully
A.N.Starlight

491313-4

Kincardine, Ont.
Jan. 5, 1935.

Hon. R.B.Bennett
Premier of Canada
Ottawa

Dear Mr. Bennett — I listened with profound interest to your Broadcast, both last night, and on Wednesday night, also. Your words
sounded most convincing and sincere.

I quite understand that a busy statesman, with the affairs of a
nation on his mind, can have little concern for the petty worries of
one family, and yet the nation is composed of individual families.

With this in mind, I feel urged to speak to you of our distress.
When you spoke of the Huron farmer you seemed to have a tender
heart (in your broadcast.) We are strong Conservatives. My husband
(George Woodstock) presided at your meeting here (in our rink) and
we afterwards had a cup of tea with you at Miss Linton's.

We mortgaged our property to put our two oldest through University. They had some brains, and were keen for the higher education, promising to return to their father, when they earned it, the
money expended. This justified the mortgage.

Fitzgerald (our son) graduated in 1932 in an Honor course in
Commerce and Finance. He spent two years in a Bank first, in order
to save some to go to college. For two years after graduation, he
tramped the streets discouraged, rebellious and completely disheartened, looking for work. All he earned, in that time was in a
Brokers (Slater and Slater) in Toronto, where he worked on an
average of sixteen hours a day, also most of Sundays, for six weeks,
and then was let off with a large number of others when business
slackened. Last March he got in another office for Twelve dollars a
week, which in July was raised to Fifteen, and now he is discharged
because the firm is discontinuing. Our daughter, an honor graduate
in English and History, also a Specialist (lacking two subjects) in
Commercial standing has been idle for years. She taught for six
months in 1932 on our High School Staff, but as the Commercial
classes were cut out, to save expense, she lost the position. She has
applied for hundreds of schools with no results. She is exceedingly
well read.

We have had Hospital and Operation bills, the past two years, staggering ones, and are "decidedly" up against it, — have borrowed on Life Insurance. We have four children. Our younger girl is in an office in Brantford, getting eleven dollars a week, paying nine dollars for Board and street car fare. She has been there for eleven months — without holidays, except 2 National holidays.

If you could be so extraordinary kind to find a job for our boy or our daughter, you would win a harrassed mother's undying gratitude.

Yours respectfully,
D. Woodstock

395125-6

Calgary Alberta

To The,
Honorable R.B.Bennett
Premier of Canada
Ottawa, Canada

Your Honor ...
Mr. Bennett, We cannot drift along in this fashion. We are three generations Canadians. I have struggled to make good citizens of my children. I cannot have my son one of the unneeded. I have had to drop insurance if I were taken tomorrow my children would not know where to turn. I am at such a critical age. I think I worry over that as well.

Perhaps you could speak one word that might place him in some station that I could feel secure for him. We'll be grateful for anything that will lead to a future ...

I am writing you personally, I do not want to appear presuming. I simply drove myself to the point, it seems so vital to me.

I trust your health may be spared. Your sane guidance is sorely needed at this terrible time, what with the Social Credit menace and

those terrible unemployed rebels roaming at large our Country needs
a firm, strong, hand — like it never did before.

We wish you abundance of health and Blessings to carry on to a
victorious finish. —

Very Sincerely Yours
Kathleen N. McKenty

83331-3

Jan 14/35
Frenette N.B.

Hon. R.B.Bennett

En vous écrivant quelque mot a légard de lasistance donner par vous
pour aider les famille sant travail mais aujourdhuit de la setuation
que nous voila rendu depuis la crisse est prie je suis obligé d'avoir de
lasistance surtou l'hiver et on est 10 de famille et je vaudrait savoir
avec asoulument rien d'autre choses et rien pour en acheté   sa me
pend audésu dun corp de farine par mois et la manier que je suis
servi il me donne une scale de $7.00 par mois un ordre et la farine
que je peux avoir pour $4.50 du corp content il nous la charge $6.50
du corp sur le chômage et le sugre que je peux avoir pour .6 cent la
livre content il nous le charge .9 c sur le chômage   la vous voyer de
quoi quie nous reste après un corp de farine a $6.50 sur un ordre de
$7.00 par mois pour 10 de famille quand que tu te leve le matin et
tait oblige de boir de leau chaude avec du pain sec et tu est oblige de
caupé le bois pour chaufé ta famille et quon a pas de linge a ce mette
sur le corp   je suis rendu a 42 ans et jai tout fait mon posible pour
ma famille   jai tou tant travaillé et je vous dit que jai jamait pati et
je travaille encore quand que je peu trouvé de l'ouvrage   mais il en a
pas et de cette manier la nous voila rendu quon fait une vit de martir
et dans ce cas je voudrait savoir si cette loi vien direct de Ottawa ou

cest la loi que les conseiler fait par aux même   jèpère que vous aller
me reponde tou de suis sur ce cas la   de vôtre tou dévoué

Claude Artoile

481903-4

Jan. the 15. 1935
Vancouver. B.C.

Premier Bennett

Dear Sir.
    You said in one of your lectures that you would give unemployed
men ten dollars a week. Oh lord i wish you would. i would be a rich
woman. my husband has been out of work four years now. he was a
bricklayers labour before on the buildings but there has been *no*
building for five years, or anything else. my husband got a little
work in the Rat Portage mill five years ago. the firm went clean out
of bussiness over four years ago. and never can get any work since. I
get an a day now and again doing day work in house for us to live on
it is hard work and i get so tired. my arms and hands pains me so
much at night. i can scarcely sleep at night. i work so hard for so
little money. my husband is a cripple has one leg. he lossed his leg in
Winnipeg Man. in 1906. with a street car. it was before they got iron
doors. he was coming home to dinner from work. the car was
crowed and he was standing near the door way. and some one
shoved him. or he lossed his balance and fell out under the car
weels while car was going. his other leg is also ingured. we did'nt
get one cent for it. they reckon it was his fault. he layed in the St.
Bonifice hospital in Norwood for ten months didnt think he would
live. I worked hard to help to pay the hospital bill. I cannot see any
prospects for my husband so many poor men out of work. and he
cannot get work so quickly as other men on account of being a
cripple and he will be 58 years old in March he dont get any pension
what soever. we both need clothes badly. I am ashamed to go out

my overcoat is so shabby. I have fixed it so much it cannot stand
fixing anymore. I havent got a deason dress to my name lord i wish
we could get a fiew dollars a week. the first thing i would buy some
clothes, as we are in rags. I was born in Mailers Creek New Brunswick. My parents died and left seven of us small children. my father
died of cancer in the face. my mother died three months later with a
cold. I was only seven years old and one sister younger. I have my
brothers and sisters married and living in St John N.B. one sister
living in Waterford, NB. my Father name was George Dupont. I
never did have a very nice life of it, it is very cold here at present and
it makes it worse for us to keep warm. Yes Mr. Bennett I would love
if you would give a dole to unemployed men if you did I would very
hard to keep you in power and get votes and will prey for you.

I am awful sorry having to write to you, but trusting you will
receive this letter and then think for the best I do hope a change will
come soon.

I Remain Yours Truly
Mrs R. Dufferin

492735-8

Little Coulee
Alberta
Jan. 23rd 1935

Hon. R.B.Bennett
Calgary, Alta

Dear Mr. Bennett,
I Would like to buy a Place & as You know it is Very hard to get
a Loan on any land now. I have no land & We are just living this
shack until I Can get a Place.

This shack We are living in has no Windows or doors. But the
owner Was Kind enough to let us move in until I could find a place.

Now I Can buy a Place for $12.00. twelve hundred dollars Cash.

It has a Nice little House 2 barns & outer buildings all fenced 76 acres. Which Can be Put in Crops in the spring.

I have no barns for my horses & I also have buy all my feed besides. Keeping a family of 6 besides my self.

I don't get relief & don't want it if I can get along without   Now Mr. Bennett I Hope you will be able to help me to get his place.

We can fix the terms to suit you on the Loan. We my Wife & I have always give you our *Vote* & will do so again.

Hope you Will be Able to help me in this matter, as the they want sell at once.

Thanking you.

Yours truly
Ralph A. Manion

P.S. Please Write Soon as we would to move out of this Cold Shack as soon as We Can. fix terms to suit your self on this land. If you care to do this we can fix the Papers in Didsbury or Carstairs

397793-4

Personal attention please
Fairville, Quebec
Jan 26th 1935

Rt. Hon. R.B.Bennett
Prime Minister
Ottawa

Dear Sir;—

I wish to call your attention to the fact that the relief administration is not fair or just in this place. The very poorest of the people very often receive less then those who are able to take care of themselves entirely. I applied a few days ago for some assistance. I was told I would have to manage the best way I could. Am I different from the other ten million Canadians. I bought a farm some years

ago on the time payment plan I have not been able to pay any on it
for four years nor taxes. This year the school board gave me a job of
15 hrs a week to enable me to pay up my tax arrears. I have let my
taxes fall behind my payments on my property slip back because I
did not want to be dependent on Gov. charity. In three years I do
not think I have received $25 in direct relief. And I think I have paid
that back in the special taxes that were applied to take care of the
Relief. It seems like politics race and creed are mixed up in direct
Relief Will I be forced on a hunger strike to get the sympathy of all
Canadians before justice will be given. I shall not rest until I have
justice myself and for others even if I have to appeal to the Governor
General I cannot see why people who have twice the earning capacity I have can get direct Relief without any trouble. While I must
manage which ever way I can. The names of these Relief Officials are
(William Grennier) Fairville, Que. Dubuq I believe head of the queer
work that is done in the Co Bonaventure Fourshet mixed up in it
some how   I wish for you to have these men brought to account for
their peculiar tricks to myself and others. Sincerely Yours

Hubert Harris

your imediate reply is requested.

484023-5

Fletcherdon Ont
29 Janvier 1935

Mr. Bennett

Cher Mr.
Je vous écrit quelque ligne pour vous demander si vous pourrier
maider pour habiller mes enfants   jes tous les misére a avoir du
relief pour manger   jes 3 enfant et jai hu 10.00 piastre pour acheter
a manger le 11 octobe et 10.00 autre piastre le 27 Novembre et

10.00 autre le 30 Janvier   il ne veule pas rien me donner et pour 5
personne il mon donner 2 fois 10.00 pour du linge   jai habillé seux
qui travaille dehor   on a coupér du bois pitoune et il veule pas
lacheter les plus jeune et moi avon presque rien pour nous vaitir et
nous devon dans les magasin et il ne veule pas nous avancer d'autre
linge ni manger   nous devon $400.00 auts piastre dans un magasin
et $80.00 dans un autre et il ne veule pas mavancer   je vous est écrit
en espirant que vous maideré jai une fille de marie et elle a 3 petit
enfant et elle a été malade au lit toute l'été et il lui on domer seulement que 10.00 de linge le premier novembe et son mari avai rien
pour s'habilé et on achéte pas grand linge avec 10.00 piastre   si vous
voulez nous envoiez pour nous 2 car nous en avon bien de besoin et
on ne vous oublirai pas dans quelque mois nous travailleron fort
pour vous

vos tout Devouez
Mde E. Vessard

398042-3

Mr. l'hon Bennett
Ottawa

Vous allez peut etre pensez que je ne suis pas frans mais ca sera le
contraire   je suis un petit garcon de 16 ans le fils dun cultivateur
vous savez comme les cultivateurs on de la misere cest annee ici   on
et une famille de 14 enfants et il y a longtemps que je peut pas allez
a lécole il faut que jaide a mon père et voila le temps arrive ou jaurais
besoin de chaussure et de linge pour mabiller   et je voudrai vous
demandez si vous voulez etre assez bon de menvoyez quelque
peastre   sa me rendrait bien service   soyez certain que sest pas
pour gaspillé   si vous pouvrez menvoyez vingt cinq piastre il me
semble que jaurait le courage de continuer a resté avec mon père et si
vous ne pourez rien je va etre obligé dabondonnez le metier
dhabitant   si cest impossible pour vous den envoyez 25 vous

menverrez ce que vous pourrez   je serai toujours contant   je nest
que 17 ans mais je vous assure que je ferai ce que je pourrai pour que
vous gardez votre place au prochaine election. Vous remerciant
d'avance.

Vous adresserez a Guillaume Duron
Linton P.Q.

jespere que vous moblirez pas sil vous plait et que vous retarderez
pas trop longtemps

398162-3

Jan 31st 1935
Cambrian Sask

Honerable Sir:—
    I wonder if you would help a poor sick woman in distress I am
sick most of the time My Husband is laid up with Rheummatism and
We Have 9 Small children the last 14 month apart Me and the child-
ren have no Shoes to Wear or any clothes of no kind Two go to
School with no coat.
    Wish you would send us a few dollars to pay necessary things the
Lord will Repay and so will I: as soon as we are able
    The Reason Im wrighting is I know you are a Wonderful Man

Hopping to hear
I Remain Your humble Servant
Mrs J.W.Gruzlewski
I thank you

[Reply: $5.00.]

398469

Isle Verte, Qué 1 février 1935

L'honnorable R.B.Bennett premier ministre

Monsieur le premier ministre.
Vous pardonnerez sans doute à une jeune écolière qui ose vous
faire perdre un temps precieux en lisant ma lettre. Alors je serai
brève. Je demeure à la campagne à deux milles de la ville d'Isle
Verte   Je suis trop loin pour me rendre au convent à pieds   il
faudrait que je serais pensionnaire. Comme mes parents sont de
pauvres cultivateurs ils ne peuvent me payer cela Actuellement je
fais ma septième année à l'école primaire mais ce n'est pas assez
approfondi pour avoir un brevet d'enseignement supérieur sans
passer par le pensionnat. Il me semble qu'instruire les enfants est
mon idéal. Quelle grand tâche de forme ces bambins qui seront peut-
être des grands hommes de demain.
Pour réaliser mon rêve il faut que quelqu un m'aide   j'ai pensé à
vous: étant célilataire vous pourez disposez vos liberalites selon votre
coeur que serais pour vous quatre cents piastres: Quelques gouttes
d'eau de moins dans la rivière et pour moi tout un monde d'avenir.
Peut-être penseriez-vous que je suis une intruse. Mais soyez assuré
que je dis la vérité   dans tout les cas vous pouvez vous renseigner
sur moi et ma famille à Mr. Forget ou bien au monastère des Ser-
vantes Jésus-Marie à Hull en vous adressant à Sr. Marie des Victoires.
Mr le premier Ministre vous pourez faire ça sans souci tandis que moi
j'ai des occupations autant qu'un premier ministre.

Donc j'espère en vous
Votre tres obligée
Germaine Tremblay

398077-8

Brazeau Alta
Feb 2nd 1935.

Mr. R.B.Bennett:—

As you were put in your present position to better the conditions
of the people, perhaps you can tell me why it is, that people who
work hard can neither have enough to eat or wear?

Lots of people who can't afford to buy thier clothing, get parcels
of clothing from churches & such like, But I have never been for-
tunate enough to get any of these and this is why I am writing you
this letter to see if you will help us.

We have never ask for relief, my husband works in the bush most
of the time, But there isnt a decent living in it. The men we sell the
timber to, get all the money. We lost our crop with hail & frost last
year, garden included, and we have some cows we are trying to
winter, as they are all we have to live on in the summer so with
buying feed & groceries for the plainest kind of a living, which I may
say is not near enough for people who have to work, and we havn't
any thing to buy clothes with and it isnt very nice to have to go out
in 50 below zero weather with hardly any cloths on.

so I want you get me a parcel of clothing from some source or
other. one thing, I want badly is a coat. I wear a size 40 bust. We
have three children ages, boy 10 yrs girl 8 yrs boy 5 yrs. any kind of
bedding would also be appreciated, as I havnt a sheet to sleep
between.

My husband is a medium sized man and one thing he needs is
work boots size 7 Now I hope you will help me out, It might restore
my faith in politicons, which at the presnt time I havn't much.

Yours truly,
Mrs. Jonathon Forester

[Reply]

Personal
Ottawa, February 19th, 1935

Dear Mrs. Forester,
I have before me for acknowledgment your letter of the 2nd of
February directed to the Prime Minister.
While Mr. Bennett receives an enormous number of appeals, I will
endeavour at an early date to send you a parcel that may be of some
service to you.

Yours faithfully,
Secretary

396217-9

Ottawa Feb 6th/35

Right Hon. R.B.Bennett
Premer of Canada

Honorable Sir
May I take the liberty of placing before you the situation I am a
present up against it is because I feel desperate and dowharted That I
am appealing to your consideration I am a widow with two girls our
only suport is what I earn by Char work. The youngest is very
delicate and still going to school. The Eldest is Stenograper but has
been unable to obtain work for a long time. Has been trying to help
out by doing house work, but the wages are very poor $2 a week I
have tryed everyone I know to help me to get work for her but I

have been unsuccessful Honorable Sir if you would kind enough to
use your influence It would be a God send to us
  I remain sir

Your Humble Servent
Helen McCracken

[Reply]

Personal
Ottawa, February 9th, 1935

Dear Mrs. McCracken,
  Mr. Bennett has this morning handed me your letter of the 6th of
February.
  I very sincerely regret I do not know of any vacancy to which I
can direct your daughter's attention. I endeavoured a few weeks ago
to make a canvass of business firms in the hope that I might learn of
some vacant positions, but I did not meet with any success. Practically all government positions, as you know, are under the control of
the Civil Service Commission, and it would be necessary for your
daughter to pass the examinations and comply with the regulations
before it would be possible for her to secure an appointment.
  Positions on the House of Commons staff were filled before
Parliament opened, and I am informed that most of those who had
employment at the House last year returned to their work this
session.
  I enclose herewith a five-dollar bill with which I would ask you to
get some little present for your daughter who is attending school.

Yours faithfully,
Secretary

395661-2

Roudeaux, N.B.
The 7th Feb. 1935

Mr. R.B.Bennett

   Dear Sir
I am writing you a few lines to ask you if you will be kind enough to
let me know the Law of the Direct Relieved, I am an Old man of
73 years old cant hardly help myself nearly cripple of both hands
and my wife 68 years old   I went to see the man who his appointed
to give the Relieved this morning and I had a hard time to get $3.00
worth   I got a bag of flour and a gallon of paraphine oil   I couldnt
not get a pound of tea nor anything else   long as we cant get no tea
we will have to eat that bag of flour with cold water   indeed it is a
hard way to live so long in the party conservative and to be used that
way. we cant even shived close for we havent got any close to shived
with [sic] nor me and the wife   we will need more grobe and some
clothing too   please let me know how long this Relieved his going
to last I wonder how it his that in some places peoples are well used
they get almost all what they need and here in Macadie they are
giving us the lest they can   I am sorry to have to send you this
complaint but I am oblige to do so but it is the first time in my live.
please answer me immediately and let me know what I have to
do   I remain your truly

Mr Federic D. Senechal

[Reply: $5.00.]

399096-9

Craven Alberta
Feb 11-1935

Dear Sir —

Please don't think Im crazy for writing you this letter, but I've
got three little children, and they are all in need of shoes as well as
underwear but shoe's are the most neaded as two of them go to
school and its cold, my husband has not had a crop for 8 years only
enough for seed and some food. and I don't know what to do. I hate
to ask for help. I never have before and we are staying off relief if
possible. What I wanted was $3.00 if I could possible get it or even
some old cloths to make over but if you don't want to do this please
don't mention it over radios as every one knows me around here and
I'm well liked, so I beg of you not to mention my name. I've never
asked anyone around here for help or cloths as I know them to well.

Yours Sincerly
Mrs P.E.Bottle

[Reply: $5.00.]

400280-1

Vitalia, Man.
Feb. 16th 1935

Governor R.B.Benitt
Outtawa Ontario,

Dear Sir:

Will you please give us some help because we are very poor
indeed. We havent got any clothes or shoes and we haven't got any
thing to sell because it is hard times. Surely some one should have
pity on us and help us. We didn't see any sugar or tea all winter and

we never had any potatoes. We can't buy any thing because everything is so dear, and we havent got any money to buy anything.

Yours truly
Mr.&Mrs. M.Krupski

398820

Vitalia, Ma.,
March 7th, 1935

Prime Minister
Ottawa, Ont.

Dear Sir,
    We thank you every so much for the present which we received a
while ago. It was of great help to us, and we got some potatoes and a
bag of flour for it. We never had such a hard life as we have now. So
once again we will thank you for the present and we wish you good
luck.

Yours truly,
Mr. & Mrs. Krupski

398827

Townsend NB
feb the 18 1935

Dear sir I am droping you a few line to let you no that I voted for
you and have a hard time to live so I am Cripple with that make it
harder for me so if I woulden be Cripple I woulden Call on you for
help I try to do the Bess I can and then vot for you again so if you

help me I would be afful glad if you could if you please and exquse
bad riting from Roderick Rouleau Jr

[Reply: $5.00.]

400455

Cap de-la-Madeleine 18 fevrier 1935

Honorable Monsieur R.B.Bennett
Prémier Ministre
Ottawa

Honorable M. Bennett.
    Il ya quelques temps, je vous adressais une lettre, vous demandant
d'être assez bon de me venir en aide —
    Et comme je n'ai pas eu de réponse je viens renouveler ma
demande.
    Comme je vous l'ai dit: je suis une jeune fille qui doit se marier
dans quelques temps et comme je ne travaille pas depuis très longtemps, je n'ai pas un sous pour acheter le stricte necessaire pour
cette occasion.
    Je viens donc encore une fois vous demander d'être assez bon de
me faire parvenir un aumône selon votre générosité.
    N'oubliez pas que nous sommes une famille de 12 dont 9 sont vos
électeurs.
    Espérant que j'aurai une réponse favorable. Je me souscris:

Votre humble servante
Camilla Bouchette

398125

Tanner Junction N.B.
Feb. 19-1935

Hon. R.B.Bennett,
Ottawa

Dear Sir:—
  As I saw your advertisment in the paper where you said you
would sec no one hungry or cold. and I am asking your assitance, as
I am both hungry and cold, and all in my care — and I have payed
my taxes for over forty year So I think the Goverment aught to help
me now. and it is up to you for to do it. if you would be kind
enough to send me a Little Help — As there is no work or no Relief
in This parish, and There are a lot in need. Of Help as Well as me —
So If you would Be Kind Enough To help me, and I will Help you
all I can — So I hope you won't Turn This Letter down But answer
By Return Mail With Good Satifation.

Yours Truly.
William E. Balford

[Reply: $5.00.]

397930-1

Gurney Sask.
Feb. 19th, 1935

Mr. R.B.Bennett
Ottawa, Ont.

Dear Sir:—
  I am coming to you for help. Because I should be wearing glasses
for over two years and my father could never afford to get me a pair
at a time like this. I try to read all your speeches but is almost

impossible because I can hardly see.

My father cannot read English so he wants me to read and tell him what you have to say but as I find it so hard to read it without glasses because I always have such awful headaches afterwards I was wondering if you couldn't send me a least twenty-five dollars so that I could get my glasses and at least a few clothes that I need very badly.

Please be kind enough and answer right away because I'd like to have a answer soon and so that I could read your speeches better. Please answer as soon as possible enclosing what I want.

My address is:

Miss Barbara Offenhauser,
Gurney

P.S. Just think of what a joy to get relief of headache for 2 years once. I am sure you would be awful glad to get help if you were in need so much. If you do not send any money answer right away. Anyway.

[Reply]

Personal
Ottawa, March 13, 1935.

Miss Barbara Offenhauser,
Gurney, Sask.

Dear Madam:

Your letter of February 19th addressed to the Prime Minister has been received.

Mr. Bennett has a great many demands upon him and has assumed heavy commitments for the assistance of many who are in difficulties at the present time. He has asked me, however, to send

you the enclosed sum of money [$2.00], which he hopes will be of
some assistance to you in obtaining the glasses you require.

Yours faithfully,
Private Secretary

398350-2

Burton, Alta
February 19/35

Mr. R.B.Bennet
Ottawa, Ont.

Dear Mr. Bennet:—
I suppose I am silly to write this letter but I havent any one else
to write to so am going to hope and pray that you will read this
yourself and help me or us, rather.
We are just one of many on relief and trying to keep our place
without been starved out. Have a good ½ section not bad buildings
and trying to get a start without any money and 5 children all small.
Have been trying to send 3 to school and live on $10.00 a month
relief for everything, medicine meat flour butter scribblers. Haven't
had any milk for 3 months but will have 2 cows fresh in March some
time. Am nursing a 10 months old baby and doing all the work
cooking washing mending on bread and potatoes some days. This is
our worst winter as my husband has had to be home to look after
the outside chores. Other winters he always made some money as we
lived in town and I could manage alone.
Am so worried on account of the children as we never have any
vegetables except potatoes and almost no fruit and baby hasn't any
shoes have kept him in old socks instead but now he is getting so he
creeps and pulls them off so often. I would like to get a couple of
little pigs this spring I am sure we can make a go of this place as its
good land and doesn't blow if we would just manage until next fall.
Just had 70 acres in last year and the dry spell just caught it right

along with the grasshoppers although we poisoned most of them there were hardly any left by fall. I cant hardly sleep for worrying about it.

My husband doesn't know I am writing this letter but I just dont know what to do for money the children come to me about everything its the women & children who suffer in these terrible times, men don't notice things. I suppose you think I am maybe making things out worse than they are but I am not. Please help me by lending me some money and I will send you my engagement ring & wedding ring as security. I know I could pay you next fall because I like this place and we have a good deal on it no interest for 10 yrs. I raised 50 chickens from 2 red hens last summer now we have nearly forty hens but they are not laying yet. If you would just lend me $50.00 even I would be the happiest woman in Alberta and you would be the best Premier of Canada because you would have been the means of saving a whole family guess I had better go to bed. My two rings cost over a $100.00 15 yrs ago but what good are they when the flour is nearly all done and there isn't much to eat in the house in the city I could pawn them but away out here. I haven't been off the farm this winter. Will expect to hear from you hope to anyway I am sure you will never be sorry any way if you do help us.

Yours sincerley
Mrs. R. Paddy

[Reply: $5.00.]

399989-91

Brechin Ont. Feb. 28, 1935

I hope you will pardon me for writing to you but I feel that, as the head of our country you should be made acquainted with some of the things we of the poorer class are up against. Oh, I know you have all kinds of this stuff thrown at you but today I just have to unload. You may recall that I wrote to you about three years ago

and you very kindly interceded for a farm loan for us at Kent, but to
no effect. We were refused the loan and the mortgage was foreclosed
and we lost everything. We made a sale to pay the taxes and I re-
served about thirty P.R.Hens that were laying and the only bit of
money we had coming in. Well, the sale day was terribly stormy and
along with other things on that day, there was a very poor turnout.
The sale amounted to $220 for what we had paid $770. and the
$220. was $24. less than the taxes. So my hens were sold at 80¢
each, which paid up the taxes and left us with nothing. When you
wrote to me you said you hoped that year would be our best. Well,
perhaps it was, It left us nothing but our experience and that has
been dearly bought. We lost $3500. – a mere nothing to some
perhaps but our life's work. We moved to the front here hoping
things might be better but since Dec. 10th, my man has been able to
bring in $3.00. He is out every day looking for work and always the
same results. Yesterday he came home and told me there is some
road work starting next week but in order to get on, the men must
sign up for relief. I wonder why men who are self-respecting have to
be subjected to such humiliation and embarrassment when they are
only too willing to work if possible. It isn't only the men who suffer
but the families of these men. We have a pair of twin boys, sixteen
years old. Both at school yet but those boys have gone all winter
without underwear and no overcoats and do not even own a suit of
clothes. They are wearing the same pants and sweaters week day and
Sunday. I have to mend and wash their pullovers so they are pre-
sentable for Sunday School but they will not go to church because
they are so shabby. We were taught to believe God put us women
here for the noble cause of Motherhood. I wonder how many would
have suffered what we have, had we known our children were not
even going to have the necessities of life. This week we have bought
just 1 lb of butter & 3 loaves of bread. I'm ashamed to ask the grocer
for any more credit. We have been eating stew. First potatoes &
carrots and then carrots and potatoes. I'm so discouraged. I wonder
which requires the greater courage, to carry on knowing how much
we are all needing and cannot have or to end it all as that poor
woman did this week in Oakville by sticking her head in a pail of
water and drowning. My last coat that I bought was eight years ago
for the fabulous sum of $10.75¢ and my sunday dress is an old one
of a cousin's made over. I wouldn't feel so badly if we only had our

home but having no prospect of ever having anything is killing me. The people around this gritty hole are saying "Wait until the new government gets in". Its all bosh. No party alone can change things much. My idea is that all must work together to accomplish much good. In trouble such as the country is laboring under now, the partyism should be forgotten for the good of all mankind. Yes, I'm tory to my toes but just the same I have no hard feelings toward those who think differently from me. Some day things will turn out all right and I am very thankful that through it all I can truthfully say I can still maintain my faith and trust in God above.

Forgive me if I have taken too much of your time. Yours respectfully,

Dorothy Franklin

400091-95

Brechin, Ont. March 18, 1935.

Hon. R.B.Bennett.

Dear Mr. Bennett, — Will you please accept my grateful thanks for the Twenty Dollars you sent me last week for the twins. I told our Minister that I had received a gift to get needed articles for them and he said he and his wife were going in to Toronto the next day and would take us along with them. I got each boy a suit of clothes and a hat for the money you sent and if you could have seen the expression of mingled pleasure and pride which overcame their faces when they got ready for Sunday School yesterday you would have been glad it was in your power to give such joy to a couple of boys.

I washed and ironed their ties and had their shoes mended and when they came to me with a kiss and "Your' a pal Mother", well, it just meant everything to me. It isn't very good grammar but it is their expression of gratitude.

I hope, Mr. Bennett, that your health will soon be restored to you.

Again thanking you and wishing you the very best of luck.

I remain
Yours respectfully
Dorothy Franklin

[See also the letter from Mrs Franklin on p. 15.]

400099-100

Maple Glen Alta
Mar 2nd 1935

Dear Sir

I am asking you for some help one way or another. I am farming west of Edmonton and I have been frozen out 2 years straight   I have a large family and this spring my wife gave birth to twin boys wich means a lot more expense before they are raised. It sure hurts my pride to do this but it is necessary.

Yours Truly
R.A. Patrick

398603

Water Springs Alta
March 5th 1935

Dear Mr R B Bennett

I am a farmers wife and come to you with great confidence. We have chozen you to guide & protect us. You have shown us, in your

generosity and ability I wish you would help me for you have the
power and means. Our place is up for taxes there is $132 against it
that means a famly of 11 will be put on the road 8 children under 15
& Baby 1 year & 1 boy 18 years my Husband 64 years old and
cripple. The Dr. has orderd more beds in my home at present they
are sleeping 4 in one bed we have no mony to buy beds & covers we
cannot get them on credit Dr said they will get T.B. if we leave it
much longer, and before time would change it might be to late   I
do want to raise heathy family   The childrens welfare is absolutely
necessary the problem is to save our home and second is get mony to
buy 4 beds & covers   We dont ask for any luxury I need hundred of
things but would not ask for them all I ask to safe guard the children
from T.B.   The amount I will leave to your Judgement   You could
put in form of a loan if times should chang we could pay it back.
The children would have something to boast in years to come hoping
to hear from you

Yours truly
Mrs Françoise Hudon

[Reply: $5.00.]

397808

Personal.
Napan Bay
N.B.

Hon R.B.Bennett

Dear Sir
    I wrote to you once before begging a little help in my time of
need, but evidently you either never rec'd it or turned it down. Now
I am writing to you again (if you will excuse pencil writing). Seeing
by the papers where you spend so much on broadcasting and
advertising, I thought perhaps you might help me out a little at this

time. My husband is a smelt fisherman on the Miramichi and altho some have done very good fishing this season his nets were not among the lucky number, and he lost three in the ice drift in Dec. Now during the past three years I have been sick a great deal, in hospital 3 times and had serious operations, these bills were very large (to me) and are not nearly all paid. Now I need doctors care again and have no means to do so, therefore I am calling on you for some help altho entirely unknown to me. We have lived thru the last 5 years of depression, and have never asked for dole.

If you can assist me in any way please do so at your earliest convenience, and please remember I would not wish my friends or any one else to know. If you have any thing to give please do so privately and you will probably never realize how much it will mean to me

Thanking you

I remain
Yours Truly
Mrs Buelah Swanson

[Reply: $10.00.]

39478-9

Tessier, Sask, March, 6, 1935

Hon. R.B.Bennett.
Ottawa.

Dear Mr. Bennett: —
I wonder if you would send me enought money to get my little brother and myself a pairs shoes and rubbers for the spring. We had no money all winter, and we have no shoes to wear   daddy cant afford to get us a pr. He had no work all winter. We live in town. We have had a pretty hard winter very little to eat, would be awful Please if you could gave us some money to buy our shoes. My

brother is 6 years and I am 12 years the 31st of March, hope I am
not asking you for too much, we will live in hopes to hear from you
soon.

from a Friend
James McLaughlin

[Reply: $2.00.]

398995

Gore Island Que.
Mar 8/35

H O N. R.B.Bennett
c/o The Senate
Ottawa Ont.

Your Highness,
    As I have had the misfortune of getting my home, and all my
belongings burnt by a fire.
    And that I am a cripple by which I have had bad luck by getting
my foot cut off and I have not been able to do any hard work every
since. I was making a fairly good living ever since by playing the
accordian on the streets until the fire burned it, and I am without it
now so I thought I would write to our Premier asking you if you
please could help me out in buying another one.
    I certainly would appreciate your kindness if you would do so.
    Wishing you the very best of luck in your coming election

I remain yours
John O'Brien

[Reply: $5.00.]

398755-6

St. Thérèse 8 mars 1935

L'honorable R.B.Bennett
Premier Ministre du Canada
Parlement. Ottawa, Ont.

Monsieur le Premier Ministre,
    En lisant le journal "La Patrie de Montreal", j'eus la surprise de
lire l'article que je vous envoie, consernant un cadeau que vous avez
fait à une petite fille de Harris Sask. C'est pourquoi l'idée me vient à
moi aussi de vous écrire pour solliciter de vous le même cadeau car je
suis un jeune garçon de 14 ans et les patins que j'ai moi aussi sont
trop petits. Comme c'est le seul sport que je puis pratiquer et que
mes parents ne peuvent pas m'en acheter d'autres, je serais bien
content si vous aurez la bonté de me faire un cadeau. En plus je dois
vous dire que mes parents sont des francs conservateurs et l'ont
toujours été. Puis comme je serai moi aussi plutard un bon conservateur je me souviendrai de ce qu'aura fait pour moi jadis un premier
Ministre Conservateur.
Esperant que vous d'aignez régarder ma demande,
Je me souscris votre humble serviteur

Michel Tessier

[Enclosure]

    M. Bennett envoie son chèque à une fillette

    HARRIS, Sask., 7. — Thelma Anderson se plaignait à ses
    petites amies que ses patins étaient trop petits. "Ecris à
    M. Bennett et il t'en enverra une paire." La petite le crut
    et écrivit au premier ministre pour lui en faire la de-
    mande. Elle vient de recevoir un chèque de $5 du chef
    du pays.

398170-1

Red Deer, Alta,
Mar. 11, 1935

Mr. Hon. Bennett,
Ottawa.

Dear Sir: —
    I am the mother of thirteen children age 50 yrs., old enough, to
know better to do what I am doing by writing you my troubles
when you no doubt have plenty to worry about, but as a mother
who fights for her children I am coming to you to see if I can get a
little help. I am not out of my head only don't know which way to
turn. We have been on relief for two years and get only $10.00 a
month to live on until this last month   I beg them for $12.50 and I
only get it in food no cash to buy any thing we need and have to
buy every thing from the store we eat. We have been able to work
out our rent until the past six months and can't pay that we are
ordered out on the 21st of this month. My husband has got a few
logs and got them to the saw mill to saw into lumber but can't find
any thing to do to get them out and they wont sell us any land to
put a shack up on, so one question I want to know is what any one
can do if we build on a flatiron piece with road going past each side?
My husband has farmed here and we did well until he was taken sick
with Typhoid Fever, since then it left him with a bad leg which
keeps him from heavy work and once in a while it is a running sore
for a month and not able to work then. He is a good husband and
father never drank, and we are both serving the Lord and it is hard
to think that there isnt some one in this old World that hasn't a kind
heart. We can't hire money now (we did when on the farm) as we
haven't any thing for security. I make over clothes for my children
to try to keep them in school, one boy is out of Grade 8 and wants
to go but we cant buy books and clothes for him so he helps his Dad
to cut wood; we try to sell some but everyone here is trying to get a
little that way so wood is cheap and it takes a long time to earn
$5.00. Is there any way you can help us to get our shack boarded in
so we can get into something and let us pay you back in some way if
any work comes. Surely something will turn up soon, it has been a
long time going this way. May God Bless you in your work; if you
don't feel you can help us it will only be another disappointment to

me and I am getting quite use to them now.
 I expect this will reach the paper basket anyway so God Bless you

I remain, Yours truly,
Mrs. Joan Brock, Red Deer.

P.S. We are trying to get a place 20 x 24 x 8 ft high.

400629-30

Gull Lake Sask
Mar 12th/35

R.B.Bennett.

Dear Sirs, —
 Im writing you to see if you could help me out a little. We are
very poor people. We just get barely enough to eat here on relief &
are not allowed any clothes now my shoes are off my feet & my
husband has no shoes or overalls to start Spring work & his underwear are in rags. We see no way where we can get any so I was
wondering if you help us out a little if we could get $10 we could
probably pay you back this fall.

Thanking you kindly
I remain
Mrs. Adam Morris

Please ans at once

[Reply: $5.00.]

398830

Chichester, Que.
March 13 1935

Dear Mr. Bennett.
    I am a little boy 11 years old I live in a very back wood place and
I am very poor there is a big bunch of us I am going to school   My
little Sister and I we have three miles to go and break our own path
but we dont mind that if we were only able to buy our books, the
Quebec books are very expensive so I just thought I would write you
maybe you would give us enough to buy our books if you dont I
Guess We will have to stop and try and earn a little money to help
out our father please excuse paper and pencil as I have no better
Hoping to hear from you real soon I am

Yours Loving Friend
Albert Drummond

Please answer soon soon soon

[Reply: $2.00.]

397812

Windsor Ont
Mar 14. 1935

Mr. Bennett.

Dear Sir.
    I am just writing a few lines to you to tell you just how I stand
I am a poor man now. I am 22 years of age and out of work. I have
walked the streets all winter trying to get work but it is no work
now. come again in couple of weeks. This is sure nice for us young
fellows. I have tried all the plants in the Border Cities. The Ford
Motor Plant but I can't even get in to talk to any of them. Mr.
Bennett I am down so fine now that I even have no good clothes to

put on Sunday to go to church. I haven't got good shoes to put on
Sunday. The relief that they give here is no good at all I don't like
it   They give pants here alright but they are made out of bran sacks.
Mr. Bennett help me out send me a suit so I can go out Sundays   If
you can't help me a little like that why never mind at all. Mr Bennett
I am writing this letter but I want you to keep this a secret all to
yourself. If you can't help me why let the matter drop and I will
make the best of it. But Please don't say anything about this
    Please help the unemployed
    I thank you

Yours truly
Edward Grant

398692-3

Trocher Alberta
March 15, 1935

Prime Minister of Canada
Premier R.B.Bennett

Dear President
    I am turning to you for help as no doubt many others have. For I
have no doubt many other people that are down and out entirely. So
Ive taken a chance on writing to you for help, expecting you can
solve our hard problem. My husband has been unable to work for a
longer time on account of poor health, I have been looking vainly
for a job but seems they are all taken, in this district. I have a
daughter over a year old. And they will not give us relief in this town
we have asked several times but cannot get any. And Premier
Bennett, Its beyond human to see your husband & daughter hunger.
So please do something about us, send us money to see us through
for near future. Till my husband gets well. I am sure he'll get a job,

as soon as farming starts. So *please PLEASE* do something to help us.

I'll be expecting an answer in the near future.

Yours truly
Mrs. L. Burdette

[Reply: $4.00.]

397815

Burt Landing Ontario
March 15/35

Mr. R. B. Bennett,
Ottawa,
Canada

Dear Mr. Bennett:
I am a girl of fifteen years who lives in the woods 25 miles west
of the town of Fort William in the district of Rainy River. We are
very poor people and are trying to get a head every day but do not
seem to be making much progress. There are six children, eight including father and mother. My eldest brother is twenty-two and has
been a sufferer of asthma since he was three years old. He cannot do
any heavy work and last November opened up a country store about
1½ miles from our home. It is a very small store as we did not have
any capital with which to start. A kind gentleman in Fort William
lent us $100. with which to buy stock enough to begin. Ever since
Richard, my brother has been getting orders of $25.00 or perhaps a
little more to replenish the little stock he has left. This way he has to
go to town nearly every day for he cannot get enough supplies to
last for many days. Whenever he is sick or when the roads are
blocked during the winter he cannot get into town and therefore the
shelves are empty. People come in and out from quite a distance to
get groceries and are often disappointed and that way we lose a lot

of trade. They often make remarks which hurt although we cannot
help it. We call the store "The New Deal Grocery"

Last year I completed my first year of High School and had to
quit, much to my regret as my plans were to take a business course.
But I have to stay home and help as we cannot afford a hired girl. I
also look after the store whenever Richard goes to town. I have very
few clothes and what ones as I have are very shabby as they mostly
were all given to me. I have only had one new coat in all my time
and that one was a very cheap one. That was when I was about 8
years old. I feel ashamed to go any place for I cannot stand to be
laughed at. My sister aged 12 and my brother aged 10 still go to
school and it takes mostly all to keep them warmly dressed and so I
have to sacrifice my clothes for them. Do not think that I do this
grudingly for I would much rather go without a lot of things than
have them go to school dressed poorly, and then be cold all the time.
I would like very much to go out and work as a hired girl as Mother
taught me how to cook and do other household duties but I am
unable to go.

My father and other brother have cut and hauled out cord wood
and pulpwood this winter which they sold to help pay our debts and
what was left to live on.

Mr. Bennett, I do hope you will not cast this letter aside with out
thinking over our situation. Please do not think I am exaggerating
for I am not. And if you could help me out a little I will not know
how to show you how much I appreciate it.

No one knows I am writing to you asking your help. If I told
anyone they would laugh and say that you would not pay any attention to my letter. Please may I ask a favour "Do not make this
publicly known".

If you are unable to help me I will thank you for reading my
letter.

I hope you are better from your illness and hope you will be able
to be up and around again very soon. If you wish to answer my
letter my address is (Miss) Emma Cotter, Burt Landing, Ontario.

Our nearest town is 10 miles away that is where we get our mail.
Thanking you again,

I remain
Respectfully Yours,
(Miss) Emma Cotter

[Reply: $5.00.]

397936-41

Moose Jaw Sask.
March 22nd/35

Premier R.B.Bennett

Dear Sir:—
    I am writing to you to see if you could help me in any way.
    I am 19 yrs. of age Mr. Bennett, but it really is impossible for me
to get work. I haven't got any shoes to wear & no coat & so I haven't
any home or any relatives here, Im all alone as it were.
    Now I tho't perhaps you could help me a little Mr. Bennett I
would be much obliged. Here in Moose Jaw it just seems impossible
to get relief unless you go & work for your board & room & I can't
work like that as I need clothes so badly. It's even a fact that not
only haven't a coat to wear but I haven't any stockings either. Mr.
Bennett if you could just help me out a little bit I would be very

pleased & would appreciate it very much & would you kindly give
me an answer.

Yours Sincerely
Barbara Harris

[Reply: Small sum.]

400391-2

Teulon, Man
March 22nd/35

Mr. R.B.Bennett
Prime Minister of Canada
Ottawa, Ont.

Dear Sir —
    I am a young mother of two small children a girl (6) and a boy
(4)   now in worst of hard times an accident happend, my girl was
playing & fell and cut her face very badley, so out off this got a
blood poison in her face, she's in a hospital now. Just at present I
have no money to pay the doctor or fare for the train to go and see
her. Of course you aren't a married man and dont know what a heart
break it is for a mother when a thing like this occur. Now Mr.
Bennett what I want to say is if you can lend me some money for a
period of 3 or 4 months when my cows will come fresh I'll turn you
the money, everybody here is broke and no where to get. I'll leave it
to you to decide how much you can lend me so please do so. I live in
Mr. H.J.Stitts consitituence (Constituuency of Selkirk).
    So please lend me some money as quick as possible. It seems to
me you'd be the best man in the world if you do so.

And a couple of dollars wouldn't mean as much as one cent
means to me. I'd make you a mortagage for horses or cattle.

Yours Very Truly
Mrs F.D.Rysnick

[Reply: $4.00.]

398697-8

Murray Harbour P.E.I.
March 24 1935

Premier Bennett:

Dear Sir:
    I am writing you to see if their is any help I could get.
    As I have a baby thirteen days old that only weighs One Pound
and I have to keep it in Cotton Wool & Olive Oil, and I havent the
money to buy it, the people bought it so far and fed me when I was
in Bed. if their is any help I could get I would like to get it as soon as
possibile.
    their is five of a family, Counting the baby.
    their will be two votes for you next Election
    Hoping too hear from you soon

Yours Truly.
Mrs Jack O'Hannon

[Reply: $5.00.]

398758-9

Teeswater Ontario
March 25 1935.

Dear Mr Bennett
   I am writing you these few lines to let you know the kind of
hardships I am in and I am wondering if you would help me out.
   I have had no work for the last three and a half years although I
have a good education I have a pair of shoes   well you cannot call
them shoes for they are just about done, one suit of clothes which I
have on my back and only one shirt and I have tried to get a job
everywhere but could not, I even tried going on the road like the
transients but I found out that wouldn't do, so I am writing you
these few lines as a plea for help, a donation of any kind, and I
would also be obliged if you would try and get or find me a job I
have three years high school education and I am twenty-three years,
old enough to vote

I remain
Yours Truly,
Mr Charles Robson

P.S. I had to borrow this writing paper and envelope and will have to
borrow stamp to mail it to you.

[Reply: $2.00.]

400001-2

Renfrew
Ont. Mar. 28, 1935

Dear Sir, —
    I am just a lad out of school and looking around for a job, and
can't find one. I am sixteen years of age. My father left us twelve
years ago and we havn't heard from him since and mother has
worked out until this winter and now I am the only one in the
family that is old enough for to do any work. We have hardly any
good clothes nothing but patches and no stockings and we haven't
any money to get anything for to wear. I have only one sister, 2
brother and mother, and I am asking will you be so kind as to give us
enough money to get some shoes stockings and clothes I thank you

Yours truly
Hugh McKinnon

[Reply: $2.00.]

397955-6

Maruel, Alberta
March 30, 1935

Dear Bennett.
    I am sick on Asthma and cannot work. I have no grain nothing to
seed, land is going to stay for nothing, everything hailed out. I lost a
horse and no money to buy one. Children are going to school 3 miles
away all the clothes are torn, and they cannot stay home. I do not
want to go on relief because I am ashamed. I'm in Canada for 30
years and only got one quarter of land and thats a poor one. I have
always been voting for conservative party and always will. So please
can you help me out a little. I read in the newspaper that you are
sick, hope that you get well I will try my best to get people vote for

you this summer. If you can please, help me out a little for few
dollars.
    Please return.

Yours truly
Wm. Currie

[Reply: Small sum.]

398499

Montréal 4 Avril 1935

Monsieur Tres H. R.B.Bennett
Premier Ministre du Canada

Monsieur
    Pardonnez-moi si je me permet de vous écrire   c'est parce que
j'ai attendu parler de votre grand coeur pour les affligers   je suis un
pauvre malade avec neuf enfants qui sont dans la misère   je vous
démanderez si vous ne pouriez pas faire quelque choses pour eux car
moi je n'en ai pas pour bien long je suis tuberculeux   mais c'est mes
enfants qui me font de la peine de laisser dans la misère comme ils
sont et très jeunes   la plus vieille n'a que quatorze ans et mon plus
vieux petit garçon n'a que onze. Je ne sais pas si ma lettre va vous
foiser mais quand j'ai attendu parlé de vous et de votre genérosité je
n'ai pas plus m'enpêcher de madressez a vous.

Votre tout devoué
Claude Leduc
Hopital Sacré-Coeur

39268-9

[Newspaper clipping and anonymous letter in the Calgary constituency file, 1935:]

GUARDS REQUIRED

Officials of the city Health department have found it next to impossible to prevent men and women carting away spoiled food from the dump at Nose Creek, Dr. W.H.Hill, M.H.O., has informed the council by letter. On several occasions sanitary inspectors herded persons away from the dump only to find that they had returned later in the day.

And there are "no signs of depression in Calgary". Some of its people living on a lower level than animals.

82736

Saskatoon Sask
April 6th

Mr. Bennit —

Dear Sir —
I hereby write you a letter and tell you how I am getting used this winter. On this so called Saskatoon relief. I aint getting enough food to eat for my wife and famley. Onley about enough for to do about four days, and as far as clothing is conserned we cant get anything for my wife and famley or myself. I have been four days down at the clothing Relief berur trying to get a pair of shoes for my wife. And I havent got them yet. I took the old ones down that she did have to show them that she rely needed them now she hasent got any thing to put on her feet she is going around in her stocking feet. If you can help us out atall we need it. That the shack we are living in aint fit

for a pig to live in. We have been trying to get out of it for over a
year, as it is cold and drafty and full of bedbugs. And the reason is
they are only paying five dollars a month. And our Landlord is
marking our rent form for eight dollars a month. And this is a thing
that you ought to know. If they are charging you for the full
amount you ought to know about it, and they have been giving us
underwight in our Groceries all winter. I would like for you to
answer this right back and tell us what you can do for us. I aint very
well at the present time I have been sick for a week or so. And I
would like to know what the returnes will be.

Yours truly
Kevin O'Malley

489662-4

April 10/35
Union Mission, Ottawa

To the Honorable Mr. Bennett Prime Minister.

Dear Sir.
    I hope you will Excuse the liberty taken in writing you You may
recall Sir, one of the Convicts whome you talked with during your
Visit to Kingston penitentiary July 24th 1934. My number was no.
7999. name, D. McConna from Nova Scota   I was Sir, on punish-
ment at the time in the east cell Block. It was an Honor indeed to
speak to you in such a place and your message to me will for ever
Stand out before me. Forget the past, look ahead to the future My
Man! and trust in God.
    I am Sir, trying to live up to your message but find it hard to do
under such trying times. I am a free man now and fully intend to
play up and play the game. While at Kingston Sir I composed a little
book. I had it Cencored by the prison athorites and also by Ottawa,
and found fit for publication. Mr. Gaudy of the Equitable Press told
me he would print one thousand copys for one hundred dollars, to

be paied in Small amounts. My Book is good Sir, and I feel Sure that
if I only Could get a little help toward printing the first thousand I
could live a desent life by Selling them.

Thanking you Sir, for what help you can give me

I beg to remain
Yours truly,
D. McConna

398928

Ottawa, Ont. April 15th, 1935

Dear Miss [Bennett's Secretary], —

I hope you will excuse the liberty taken in writing you so soon
after my interview with you. You were so good, so kind, so
motherly toward me that I feel I am committing a sin by asking you
for further help, but I feel sure you understand me in every way. As
you already know about my meeting Mr. Bennett at Kingston
Penitentiary when he visited there July 24th, 1934, Mr. Bennett told
me then to come and see him when I got out, but unfortunately he
was ill and I could not see him. However, you did not forget me and
asked me in your letter of March 1st to come and see you, which I
did and, am more than glad of the way in which you received me. I
was so impressed by your kindness I just had to send you a flower to
express my thoughts.

The Ten Dollars you gave me for food had to be used for the
printing of my book, which I am more than glad to tell you that it
went to press Monday, the 8th. Mr. Gaudy of the Equitable Press is
printing the first thousand copies for One Hundred Dollars, after
which it will be much cheaper. I may say that I have had to deprive
myself of a good many things in order to have my book printed, but
it is well worth it because I can make my own living then. My book
should be finished about two or three weeks from now, and as I have
invested the Ten Dollars you gave me, I am asking you, "Shall I say
loan, Mam (?) of another Ten Dollars to pay my room and meals
until my book is printed. I could get along by the orthodox way of
the unproductive gentleman of the road, but I know you do not

wish me to do this.

I hope you will pardon me for what I did, but I just could not help it. I felt so grateful for what you had done for me, I even had to write home and tell them about it.

I might state that my clothes are in a bad state of repair and rather than call on you in such a state I am asking you Mam, if you would please send me a letter, and when I get better clothes I will come and see you,

Yours faithfully,
Mr. D. McConna
Union Mission
Ottawa, Ont.

P.S. Please phone Mr. Gaudy of the Equitable Press and ask him if he thinks my book will be a good seller.

[Reply]

Ottawa, April 16, 1935.

Dear Mr. McConna:

I have been hoping to write you a letter with my own hand to thank you for your kind gift of flowers and for the little poem which you enclosed. I have been so desperately pressed with work, in view of the fact that Mr. Bennett will be leaving shortly for the Old Country, that I trust you will accept my apology for not having been able to do so. I do not yet know by whom Mr. Bennett is to be accompanied, but if it is not necessary for me to leave the City I will be glad to see you again at an early date.

Under the circumstances, I feel sure you will forgive my not having been able to speak to Mr. Gaudy as your letter suggested. I am enclosing a five-dollar bill and I hope that your book will be in

every way a complete success in order that you may re-establish
yourself, as you appear to be so anxious to do.

Yours faithfully,

398930-1

April 11/35
Sask. Canada

Monsieur le premier Ministre
    Vous allez peut être me trouver audacieux de vous écrire cette
lettre mais si je prends cette permission c'est le besoin qui me force à
le faire; voici mon cas: Je suis un pauvre fermier de l'ouest; qui a
subi l'invasion des sauterelles et ensuite la sécheresse dont je suppose
vous avez entendu parler. Par suite d'efforts et de privations je suis
parvenue à me suffire et à faire vivre ma famille jusque maintenant
sans aucun secours mais voila que toutes mes resources sont épuisées
et je me suis adressé aux bureaux du Relief où il me fut répondu
qu'un conservateur comme moit devrait s'adresser directement à Mr
Bennet. Comme vous pouvez voir Mr le premier Ministre ce n'est
qu'à cause que je suis du Parti conservateur que tout secours m'est
refusé   cependant j'en ai grand besoin car il fait un froid bien dur
ici et je n'ai pas d'argent pour acheter un peu de charbon et mes
enfants ne sont pas assez nourris ni vêtus. Trouvez vous cela juste? Je
sais que j'ai fait beaucoup de propagande pour le parti conservateur;
c'est pourquoi les libéraux me refusent du secour mais je ne regrette
rien encore, car j'ai confiance à votre grande générosité et j'espère
que vous ne me laisserez pas plus longtemps dans cette affreuse
misère dans laquelle je me trouve.
    J'ose espéré que vous ne rejetterez pas ma demande et que vous
daignerez m'envoyer une petite satisfaction

C'est dans cet espoir que je reste toujours votre dévoué serviteur conservateur.

Robert Jules Picard

489826-7

Dempster Sask.
April 15, 1935

R.B.Bennett Esq.
Ottawa
Ont

Dear Friend —
    I just can not stand for our treatment any longer without getting it off our chest. We came out here in Aug 1932 from Saskatoon on the Government Relief Plan. So you will understand that we have practically nothing as we had very little to start on, and we have worked very hard but have had terrible bad luck. We have lost 3 horses since coming out here so now are stranded with one horse which is on last legs. So how is it possible to go ahead and farm without help from somewhere. Last spring we had a neighbor break some for us. We have 15 acres now broke here, and my husband was working nearly all summer to pay the neighbor back so that certainly isnt going to put us somewhere we are going back fast. Still we are working like slaves, never have enough to eat and very little to wear. We have 5 children and our 2 selves. My baby was born up here without help of doctor or help in the house. Only what the neighbors felt like helping out. Now she is 16 month old and doesn't walk mostly lack of proper food. The other children all boys have been sick this winter, but how would it be possible to be healthy in such a condition. Last August our relief was cut down to $8.25 a month, but since Jan have recieved $11.65 so you see it is imposible to give the children proper foods. We had no garden at all everything froze to the ground as soon as it was started growing. We have about

20 chicken 1 cow. no meat or potatoes only what we buy many a
meal around here is dry bread and milk when our cow is milking
otherwise its water, butter is an extra luxury which we cannot
afford. None of us have proper footwear now its not fit to be outside unless clothed properly. Its is a sin and a shame to be in such
circumstance as that. It sure does grieve one when there nothing to
eat or wear. We loan settler from the city's do not seem to be treated
as well as those that moved in from the dried-out areas as they are
fully equiped with live stock and also machinery, where we have
nothing. I sure would like to know why that is. You maybe able to
understand how it would be possible to feed our family on less 2½
cents each person each meal it is quite impossible as I have tried
every way of getting by. But cannot make it go. My family don't live
anymore we only exist. I think if the situation was more clearly put
to the right parties they could help us more some less, as there are
people who have cattle, garden, and could get by without gov. help
still they recieve assitance which does only makes it worse for those
who really need it. I am looking forward that you may be able to
help us in some way. We most certainly would like to be on the
upward road. Just think how many familes in these north woods are
starving, trying to make things go. Such hard work without food to
supply body energy. So first the body fails then the mind. I know
Im very near a nerbous wreck. If we were allowed supose the doctor
would tell me I had a nervous breakdown as it is I have to keep
trudging along trying to make the best, but don't think I can stand
the strain much longer. We never get out amongst any kind of enter-
tainment as relief people are not allowed any recreation of any kind.
We would be so thankful to you if you could help us in some way.
Today is only the 15th of the month and our flour is all gone
already and the stores will not give any credit out. So we'll all be
quite hungry untill the first of the month. Please give this your
personal consideration and send me an answer of what could be
done we are practally at the end of our rope now. Thanking you
again for your attention.

Your Faithfull Servant.
Mrs Otto Brelgen

489833-6

May 13-35
Calgary

When you went in for
Premier I voted (also my
hubby.) for you. Please
see if you help me.

Premier R.B.Bennett
Ottawa

Dear sir As it is 4 oclock in the morning & I cannot sleep for
worrying weeping over financial worries I decided to drop you a few
lines to let you know how bad I feel altho words will never be able
to explain my grief. One has to have grief them selves before they
can realize what another is going through. And you are not worried
with the likes of this for I realize you have Plenty. Anyway I am
writing in kind words. I am truly a sick woman. I have been for a
few years but I am getting worse and the terrible financial worries
are not helping but surely making it worse. I have been fighting
against worry untill I feel as I am going to break down completely ... I have a very poor education other wise I would write you
a nicely composed letter. I am very economical I bake all my own
bread and use the flour bags for making undies for my little girl.
There isnt a thing wasted in my house, and I couldnt get my rent
light gas & water cheaper no matter how I tried. But I will have to
move in the fall for this place is sold, and I am sure it will cost me
more then. Now please dont throw my letter away without reading
it. I would be filled with joy if you would give these few lines your
good consideration and that is to please allow me more to finance
with or at least please provide for medicine for me & kiddies $10.00
or $15.00 would help me in lots of ways in my health especially.
You may get in contact with Drs. McEachern J.S. & Dr H.N.Jennings

of Calgary, they can tell you whether I am sick or not. I wont ask you to take my word.

Sincerely.
Mrs. Rose Artimus

P.S. I am a widow with four kiddies.

83193-6

Calgary, Alberta
May 17th, 1935

Hon. R.B.Bennett
Prime Minister of Canada:—

Dear Sir:—
    Yesterday the city came and turned of my water supply.
    My home is my only means of existing. I have 3 boys any one of them will be more than glad to do any kind of work to pay, but the foreigners seem to be only ones to be able to get work. Now can the city close my home for my water bill of $11.60?
    I ask no relief simply work for my boys who are quite capable. The Second is a good Boss for any gang of workers and has always been use to that line of work. They are willing to do any honest work.
    Thanking you in advance,
    Very sorry to have to bother you,

Yours truly
Jennifer McGillvery

83205-6

Regina Sask.
May 24/35

Hon. R B Bennett.
Prime Minister of Canada

Dear Sir:
    You will. no doubt be surpriced to recived this requaist. Now, I
have been thinking that you bcing premier
    I thought that you would have second hand clothing that would
not be suitable for you to wear. as I am straped for clothes fit to
wear to Church I disided to write to you
    My best suit is over 8 years old and pretty well frayed
    Judging you by your picture I beleve you are about the same size
as myself
    I am 49 chest measure
    now. if your clothes are not large enough. perharps you will know
of another conservative Freend that would have what would suit
    I might say my peoplc and I have allways been stunch Conser-
vatives I would'nt ask a Liberal party if I had to go naked.
    I was 69 years of age May 22/35
    I voted as a farmer's son when I was 18 years old for Sir John A
McDonald's Goverment and Im still on the list
    Now. it is not becouse I vote for your party that I am asking this
requaist but I gave in application to the City relief clothing Dpt last
fall and they told me they dident give outside clothing atall if you
can help me out please keep it confidential and oblige

I am yours respectfuly
J.A.Graydon

[Reply: $5.00.]

400517-8

North Bay, Ont. May 27/35

R.B.Bennet Es.
Ottawa, Ont.

Hon Sir:—
It is with reluctance that I write you, but through circumstances of
unforseen misfortune and calamity, I find myself reduced to the
lowest depth of poverty. I was hoping you could get me a small
portion of that fund for cancer patients I am in desperate need of
150.00 right now, to pay rent and keep my home together for the
short time my wife has to live here.

  She has had two operations and radium treatments for her cancer
and now the Dr. tells me it is working up to her brain and there is
not a thing that can be done for her, only give her something to
deaden the pain. I owe a hundred dollars for rent and another 50.00
for groceries and drugs. You see I am one of the men who should of
gone on releif three years ago but did not, my pride has kept me of
relief and now I find myself just about to be thrown on the street
with a dying wife on my hands. My landlord has told me either to
pay up or he is going to send the sheriff down befor long. Cleaning &
pressing business slow. Can they turn a man out with a sick wife. I
am a tailor by trade and it is one of the trades that has been killed in
the past few years by machinery. I am past 60 now and to old to
change. If you can get me a hundred and fifty dollars of that cancer
fund money it sure would help me over the tough spot now. If you
wish to write Dr. G.E.Richards at the Toronto Gen. Hospital, who
has charge the department of Radiology. He can tell you all about
my wife's case and to prove, I am not trying any trick. I enclose his
last letter to me. My wife is suffering terrible pain in the head arm
and shoulder and Im afraid cannot last long. How I will ever give her
a decent burial when she goes is beyond me. However that dont
mater now. It's only to keep her comfortable that matters and

supplied with drugs. Trusting your health is better and you can do something for me, I am

Yours truly
T.H.Stevens

[Reply: $10.00.]

398770-1

Fanta Sask.
May 27, 1935

Dear Mr. Bennett.
    Here I come with my story to you, I had a bad misfortune latly my house burned down and everything in it nothing was saved, my husband burned himself too which he is very sick. will you please help me out a little, our flour burned too, Please answer with some help as I need flour bad and clothing.

Thank you.

Your truly.
Mrs Max Gnoinski

[Reply: $5.00.]

400303

Weyburn
Sask
Jun 1

Dear Mr.Bennett: —
   Just a line if you will receive it, I am glad to learn you are well
again and that you were able to go to Englan seaing you pictue and
how they welcome you at docks when liner, how rushing welcome
on your returne and I all so wish you may yeas a helth and strength
as we ned you. You alys get my voat and my famely two we are in
one of thoes dried out places for tree years, we are looked after by
the municipaliy for eats but I am verey short of clothing and other
things, I will be 25 years married on June 11
   You will have my voat allys and how I love to read of what you
are doing for people of the world, I am at present vey much in nead
of money, but god will provide I will still watch for you write ups in
paper wishing you meny helthy day

Your Friend
Mrs C.R.Gray

(P s, just burn this)

[Reply: $5.00.]

400174-5

Vancouver, B.C.
June 2nd, 1935

Dear Mr. Bennet;
   Ever since I can remember I have had the ambition to play a
violin. I have been promised one over and over again. Now my father
has had no employment for over three years, so hopes of ever own-
ing one are practically gone.
   My father not understanding what it would mean to me, declares

I am too old to learn. As I am only just nearing my seventeenth
birthday I'm positive I could still learn with determination and
patience. But I can't without the instrument and I thought maybe
you could sujest something. Will you please try?

I see others with violins who don't seem to appreciate them,
when I've been yearning for one all my life.

Sincerely
Sylvia Prior

[Reply: $10.00.]

398613-4

Winnipeg, Manitoba
June 3rd, 1935

Dear Sir:—

I am one of the many citizens throughout this country who has
the misfortune of being unemployed.

We are at present on City Releif which we have been forced to
accept during the past 62 months.

We have four children whom are not in good health because I am
not able to provide for them in the proper manner.

I myself am in fair health and physically able to work at practically any class of work if I could get it to do.

I will mention the class of employment that I am able to do in a
first class manner.

In Telephone Service I am able to work in many branches on
several types of systems.

In Railway Telegraphy and Telephone service I can do any repair
work that may arise either line work, Instruments and all other
apparatus or equipment.

In other electrical work I am qualified but at present do not carry
a license.

Our children are in need of clothing and in general we are badly in need of further help than we at present are able to obtain. My wife is in very poor health and I am unable to do anything to assist her to secure health.

What we really need is help preferably in the nature of some permanent employment.

I am not a total stranger to you personally as I have met you years ago in Calgary while you were actively engaged in law work in that city. Therefore I appealling direct to you to assist me if you so wish.

A suggestion if you would care to accept it is. Will you be so good as to discuss this matter of employment with whatever acquaintances that you may have. Hon. R.J.Manion and Mr. E.W.Beatty of the Can. Natl. Rail and the Can. Pac. Railways respectively are both in a position to authorize my employment in a district somewhere on Maintenance work.

Personally in reading our newspapers I am sure that you are doing all that is humanely possible to do to rectify conditions and we have you and our Government to thank that things are not worse than they are.

Would you care to Help Ye One Another for the sake of my family more so than myself.

I trust that I may be worthy of your co-operation to secure some employment anywhere doing anything.

Thanking you in anticipation I remain,

Yours very truly
Charles Grierson

[See also letters from Grierson on pp. 22, 46, 68, 156, 161, 172.]

396065-7

Chadwick
Ont June 15, 1935

Dear Sir: —
   No dought you will be surprised to receive this letter I have been
advised by a friend of your's to write you in so doing I am asking
you to Please not let this be Known in Public as my husband doesn't
like me to ask for help from any one we have had so much sickness
in our family the last 9 yrs. and specially the last seven months I
havn't been able to do anything for nearly seven months having a
real serious operation my heart has gone bad my two girls 10. and 12
yrs old have both be sick since Feb. under medical treatment I have
not the money to give them or myself the medicine we should and
we are all in much need of clothes if you have any suits or clothing
for men you have given up I wish you would send some to us or if
you feel you could send me a little money to help for some clothes
for the girls I am sure I would feel very thankful for it if you knoew
how hard we have tried and how much sickness and trouble we have
had I am sure you would help us some if you send anything in Parcel
or money send it direct to me I am sure I will make the best of
it Possible our address is Mrs. Stewart Nolan Chadwick Ont either Post
office or express. May God bless you in your Service I might say we
are on a farm, doing our best.

[Reply: $5.00.]

398776-7

Toronto Mens Hostel
Toronto
16th June 35

Dear Mr. Bennett
in company with lots of others, whom the depression has hit, I am
asking you decide a Bet political arguments are high here. The

argument in question was this — that you would not buy a man a
pair of Shoes, if you saw one without them. I said I bet you would if
it was genuine. The reply was well you have not got a decent pair try
him I replied I will bet you my half dozen medals that he would —
As regards my citizenship and a good soldier & Conservative I refer
to you Col Reg Geary M.P., KC Major W. Heighinton MPP KC whom
I served under overseas so I hope you save my medals from this —
Red —

Yours very truly
Sgt Mr Stephen G. Pindle DCM etc

[Reply]

Personal and Confidential
Ottawa, June 19th, 1935

Dear Sir,
    I have before me for acknowledgment your letter of the 16th of
June directed to Mr. Bennett.
    If you were in Ottawa I could show you a list, that would surprise
you, of those to whom Mr. Bennett has given assistance. The very
number of requests precludes his giving a large amount to any one,
but, as this is a matter handled by me personally, I may say that I
have attended to many, many hundreds. Mr. Bennett does not
advertise what he does in the way of financial service. One difficulty
I face is, in May last I gave some money to a couple of men who are
in the hostel here with the result that I immediately had some thirty
others come in for like assistance, and one man even came down
from Peterboro. As I had then exhausted the sum I had available, it
may be that one or two applicants did not have their appeals met. It
would be utterly impossible for any one person to meet all the
demands that are made upon Mr. Bennett, and very often those who
are most generously treated are the ones who have least
appreciation.
    I gather from your letter that you are appealing for a pair of
shoes. I therefore enclose herewith a two-dollar bill, but I prefer that
you keep this matter confidential in view of the fact, as I have said,

that Mr. Bennett does not make capital out of his generosity. I do not propose to contribute shoes to men like the friend with whom you have the bet, merely because they ask for them. There are too many people in Canada who appreciate their appeals being met to bother with those who do not. If you will send me the name of the man with whom you have the bet, I will be glad to have it.

I note your letter states that you served overseas under Colonel Geary and Major Heighington.

Yours faithfully,
Secretary

400019-20

Calgary June 18th 1935

Dear Mr. Bennett,
Do please raise the Old Age Pension to at least thirty dollar per month. So many of your very old friends, myself included, have really not enough to exist on.
Very best wishes for your good health,

Sincerely,
Alma Ward

83286

Winnipeg, Manitoba
June 18th. 1935

R.B.Bennett
Ottawa, Ontario

Dear Sir:—

I have been expecting a reply to a letter I sent to you personally
on June 3rd. 1935.

Is it possible that this has been set to one side as not being
worthy of consideration.

The contents were to ask your assistance to obtain employment,
which is very necessary to me at this time.

I have been unemployed for over five years and as there are Six
persons in our family it is essential that I secure work immediately.

Do you personally know what it is too be hungry and to have
your children pay for your not being able to provide for them. The
answer is no you have never heard a child ask for things that you
cannot give them. Have you?

Won't you be friendly enough to assist me through your connections to obtain employment.

Hon. R.J.Manion is in a position to authorize my employment
with the Canadian National Railways in the Telegraphy Department
or otherwheres.

Sir E.W.Beatty is also in a position to authorize my employment
with the Canadian Pacific Railways in the Telegraph Department or
otherwheres.

Mr. Sims of the Dominion Government Telegraphs is also in a
position to employe me.

The only reason that I am unemployed is that I am not connected
in any way to these men.

Would you please spare a few moments at your convenience and
discuss my case with them individually. You cannot have the faintest
idea of what it would mean to me to secure employment.

I have mentioned these departments because I am fully experienced in the construction, operation and maintainence of them and
have suggested them so that if I obtain the chance that I will have
the knowledge to make use of my experience to be beneficial to
both parties.

I do not wish to write often to you as I cannot afford to spare the
money for stamps but I do beleive that if you wish to help a man
that is down and you sincerely wish to, that you will see that I
secure employment of some nature at an early date doing something
at any location.

For your information I have had a number of years experience in
handling Electricity in many forms such as Constructional work,
operation and maintainence.

Have also a Seaman's Certificate, Chaueffers license.

Am 34 years of age and one of Canadas Citzens.

As they say "WE WANT BREAD" such is the case with our
family, we not only want, but are in dire need of more to maintain
health. At the present releif issue our children will be mere frames
when they become old enough to go out for themselves. My wife
and I have really forgotten what a real square meal looks like let
alone taste like.

If you are in doubt drop in sometime and eat a meal with us I
guarantee that your first stop would be to a restaurant and make up
for what you went without.

So would we if we were able to. But there is the difference you
can but we cannot.

Will you help me to get into the position where we can do this
independently. If so please do so at once.

At the present time you are in a position to assist me. Who knows
that the position may someday reversed.

I met you, many years ago when the position you now hold was a
long way off. A few years makes a considerable difference so it
seems.

I trust that this letter shall not be misconstrued by you other
than from one requiring immediate employment to prevent his
family from becoming incapable of existing.

Please.

I am,
Yours very truly,
Charles Grierson

[Reply]

Ottawa, June 21st, 1935

Dear Mr. Grierson

I have before me for acknowledgment your letter of the 18th
June, directed to the Prime Minister.

Have you made formal application to the Canadian National
Railways for employment? Honourable R.J.Manion is Minister of
Railways and Canals but all staff employed by the Railway Com-
pany is appointed and is under the complete control of the operating
officials of the Railway Company. Have you also made an applica-
tion to the Canadian Pacific Railway for employment? The Canadian
Pacific Railway is a privately owned railway and no suggestion that
Mr. Bennett could make would be of any service to you as the
Company officials employ their staff after receiving applications and
only when they have available vacancies.

Have you made application to the Dominion Government
Telegraphs? If you make a formal application for employment and
thereafter so advise me I shall speak to Mr. Sims on your behalf,
although I do not know whether this will be of any service to you as
the Department is also in the position of only employing such staff
as they require.

Government positions are, for the most part, under the control of
the Civil Service Commission and it is necessary for you to write the
examinations and comply with the Regulations before an appointment can be made under the Commission.

I have recently made a survey of business firms with the hope of
finding some vacancies to which I could direct the attention of those
who write Mr. Bennett, but, up to the present time, I have not met
with success. Business firms appear to be giving first opportunity to
those who were previously in their employ with whose services they
had to dispense. In the meantime, I enclose a $5.00 bill which may
be of some little service to you in securing something for your
children.

The Dominion Government has let contracts for certain public
works, some of the buildings being constructed in Winnipeg.

Mr. Bennett is so desperately pressed with work in the House that it is practically impossible for him to deal with his correspondence. I trust, therefore, you will accept this acknowledgement of your letter.

Yours faithfully,
Private Secretary

[See also letters from Grierson on pp. 22, 46, 68, 151, 161, 172.]

396068-72

Weidon, Man.
June 18, 1935

Mr. R.B.Bennett
Ottawa, Can.

Dear Sir:
  I am down and out, have tried all means to dip up an existence during this crisis, but failed. I am 22 and willing to live — will you please help.
  I am parentless and desperate, have no one to appeal to.

Sincerely Yours.
G.R. Scott

396116

Sayward, Vancouver Island
June 28/35

Hon. R.B.Bennett.
Prime Minister.
Ottawa, Canada.

Dear Sir:—
   Please Pardon me for Writing you. but I am In Such a Circumstances That I Really dont Know What to do. When Will This
Distress & Mental Agitation Amongst the People come to an End. &
how Long Will This Starvation Last. I am on The Relief & only Git 4
days Work on The Public Road at $3.20 per day. Amount $12.80. I
am a Married Man & That are not Sufficient For both of us to Live
on. Next Came My Land Taxes of 3 years. The Mount of $12.50. If I
dont Pay it This year. Then The Government of B.C. Will Have My
40 acres Canceled. & I & My Wife Will be on The bear Ground. is
That Way The Government Will Help The Poor Men. I have Tryed to
Borrow The $12.50 From People here. but it is Impossible to do so.
I am a Willing Worker & have a Good Health at My age of 69 years
do not Drink Intoxicating Liquor. Would you Please Give Me any
Information How or What to do. I am Thanking you in Anticipation.
a Peaceful Man.

Yours Very Truly
Lawrence Knutman

400565-6

Farmingham Sask.
June 29 1935

Dear Mr. Benett:—
   I shall now begin to tell you what I am about to ask you. I have
just finished school for my summer holidays. I have managed to pass
the grade eight Standard Examination tests which were forwarded

by the Dept. of Education in Sask. I am now sixteen years old and I to continue school if possible. Their is three of us in our grade, and none of us can afford to buy the books which are necessary to continue in grade nine. If we could manage to get one set of books, we could all work together. And in that way it would be possible for us to manage. But the crops are so poor and the money so scarce, that we cannot even do that. So I decided to drop you a line, to see if it would be possible for you to give us a hand. If so I shall be very grateful to you. If not we shall all have to remain at home.

Your's Trully
George Roley

[Reply: $4.00.]

400181

Winnipeg, Manitoba
July 2nd, 1935

Private Secretary
Prime Minister's Office
Ottawa, Ontario.

Dear Sir:—
I received your letter dated June 21st to-day and also the sum of five dollars.

The enclosure was very much apprecated and I am afraid that you personally did misconstrue the intentions as meant in my letter. It was with the intention of securing employment that I wrote the letter and not to secure personal financial help.

However if you personally are able to afford the amount you sent I wish to thank you very sincerely for the assistance as it came at a time to partially save us as I shall explain later in this letter.

In this letter I shall try to explain further to your reply and to clarify my position to you.

I appreciate that the Prime Minister has considerable matters on his hands at this time and in view of that I am grateful for an answer even though indirect. I would also appreciate if my letter did reach him that you call his attention to the fact that I am one whom is willing to work if I can possibly find it.

Regarding to making application to the Canadian National Railways. I have already done so and have secured a few days work spread over a period of one year. It was in the Telegraph Dept at Winnipeg. Starting July 16th-1934 I received 9 days work. In November I received a few more days but that is all I have got from them. 20 days would more than cover the amount of time that I worked there. To-day I learned that they have during the month of June sent out three gangs of men possibly totally 30 or 40 and there are one or two whom are new men and this is their first time employed by them. These men have been sent out through friends whom are acquainted with those in authority, and men with seniority are still in town waiting to be called. It was with this in mind that I mentioned in my previous letter asking Mr. Bennett to take the matter of employment up with Hon. R.J.Manion. Being a Government Railway his word would carry a quite a peice I fully beleive.

In regard to making application with the Can. Pac. Railway I have also made application to them and have been successful in getting just a few days here and there in fact about 10 days only when they really needed men badly in storm work. They too follow the same rules of friendship which makes it hard even though a man has plenty of experience and willing to work. Such conditions can only be met with the same methods as they all use now-a-days. If a man has good connections then he will get a goodly portion of work. It does not seem to matter whether a man actually has experience or not if he says he can do it they send him out. If he makes a number of mistakes he is able to be covered up because the man in charge will not take a chance in reporting him because he knows that he got on the job through friends.

In winter when we have sleet storms these men are elsewhere and then is the only time that an experienced man stands a chance. Because experience has taught him how to climb an ice covered pole and how to handle himself when at work. But even at that there are many good men out of work and many men holding jobs through false security rather than actual experience.

In reference to making application to Mr. Sims. I had sometime ago made application to him by letter but was unable to secure employment at that time. I have to-day written him another letter a copy of which I enclose for your convenience.

Regarding the contracts which have been let for Winnipeg, I have discussed the possibility of employment personally with Mr. W.H.Carter of Carter Halls Aldinger but have not met with much success.

In all I have over 1300 applications for employment in Winnipeg and elsewhere and to these places I constantly go periodically to remind them I am still seeking employment. In fact I have a box 10" x 4" x 30" in size in which I have several hundreds of letters in reply to my quests for employment.

I have tried during my period of unemployment to contact some honorable means of living but to be very frank I am getting disgusted.

I have devoted some of my time to new devices which I beleive would be worthy objects. Some of them may appear other than sensible to you. One of them is a device to go on the dash panel of a car. The object is to notify the driver immediately if any of the lights are not working. It takes care of the headlights, taillights and all other lights. It would be a real safety measure to have on all cars as a great many accidents are caused by insufficient lights. The actual cost is small in quantity considerably under $1.00 to produce. It would take possibly $500.00 to get protection (Patents etc) and make a demonstraton and enough units to place on the market. There are several hundreds of thousands cars on the North American Continent and every one of them should have it. These could be marketed for 2 to $2.50 installed and would create a real income to the makers. I have written to many manufacturers of cars & accecories and they want models etc before they discuss the matter further.

I will not take up your time explaining them all though I have drafted plans for several devices which are equivalent in usefullness to the one mentioned above. Among them is a device to protect a Battleship from torepedos. An airplane motor with an auxilary cylinder and emergency ignition system. An Electric Ray which will deflect the course of a bullet at a range from 6" upward.

These devices are not nightmares but actually sane & feasible theories once they are explained on paper and in demonstration of use.

The enclosure of money that you kindly sent to us is the first actual money that we have had in our hands since November 1934 which totalled more than 50 cents. Some months ago we were desperate for some furniture such as beds & chairs etc. and I got some from a local store on terms so much down and so much a month. Well we are considerably in arrears and they intended to repossess the same to-day and came to do so at the same time the mailman arrived with your letter. The furniture totaled to $100.00 when we first received it and there is $80.00 owing on it at this time. Therefore there was nothing else to do but to give the money to them in the hope that somehow or other I may get employment in the next few days so that I'll be able to pay them some more otherwise we will be on the floor to sleep and eat so I beleive that you can readily see that the money was put to good use. We did however get a dollar's worth of groceries which will be very useful.

To make matters more complicated our whole family have a bad case of Whooping Cough and the kiddies are very sick at this time.

I am enclosing a picture which was taken by a friend whom we visited a short time ago. I am sending it to you so that you shall see the little group that I am trying to make it more pleasant for them. If you care to keep it you are surely welcome to it and if not please do not throw it away but return it to me. This *only* if you have no use for it.

I worked for the Manitoba Telephone System under Mr. J.E.Lowry for sometime and I lost my position on February 25-1930 through being guaransheed which at the time I could not prevent. It was very bitter to lose this job as I loved my work there and every employee were friends. It may be possible for me to be reinstated if it were taken up from the proper source. Possibly you may care to take the matter up for me. Hon. W.J.Major is Minister of Telephones at Winnipeg and Mr. Lowry is Commissioner of the Manitoba Telephone System a subsidary of the Provincial Government. I myself I cannot seem to convince them of my sincerety of good faith.

I did not intend to write such a lengthy letter but as I have done so I trust you will feel that in appreciation for what you have done for me that I wanted to give you an explanation which I beleive is due to one, whom would help one, that is sincere at heart.

Thanking you I am.

Yours very truly,
Charles Grierson

[Reply]

Ottawa, July 8th, 1935

Dear Mr. Grierson,

I have your letter of the 2nd July, and I have communicated with Mr. Sims on your behalf. I do not know, however, whether this will be of any service to you.

I do not personally know Honourable W.J. Major, Minister of Telephones at Winnipeg but I have had a friend of mine who does know him personally communicate with him. I presume his ability to employ you depends entirely upon whether or not he has any vacancy to which you could be appointed.

As the snapshot included in your letter is the only one you have I am returning it to you herewith as there does not appear to be any object in retaining it on the files here and you may require it to show to someone else. I can understand your anxiety to secure employment to take care of your nice little family. Under the circumstances mentioned by you I enclose a further $5.00 bill with which perhaps you could secure some little present for the children.

Yours faithfully,
Secretary

[See also letters from Grierson on pp. 22, 46, 68, 151, 156, 172.]

396073-81

Rutland, B.C.
July 5, 1935

Dear Mr. Bennet.
    Would you be so kind as to give me a new bathing suit and cap so
that I would be able to go in swimming in the Okanogan Lake?
Times are so hard in the fruit district of the Okanogan Valley, we
children don't get any luxuries as our parents have no money for us
to spend.
    Hoping to hear from you, I remain —

Your sincere little friend,
Inga Nopper

[Reply: $2.00.]

400106

Aberdeen, Sask.,
July 6th 1935

Dear Sir.
    I am writting you these few lines asking you your advice or a
little help as we are dead broke, between sickness and depression
these last six years. We had a little business in groceries and confec-
tionery. We then bought the building and we paid for it and now it
has been sold for taxes so we will be homeless in two months time as
we cannot redeem the place and as you know the work is very hard
to get so in March we got word that there was work in Timmins Ont.
so my husband managed to get money from the council which
amounted to fifteen dollars, to get down there and so far he has got
nothing. He has got one day's work in three months and I got a
letter from him the other day and he says he is penniless and cannot
get home. Every place he goes they say that he is too old to work

and he has heart trouble which makes it worse. We have four children nearly without food and cloths.
    Thanking you for your trouble,

Yours truly
Mrs. C. McKie

Please answer this letter as we are one of your supporters.

[Reply: $4.00.]

399004

Welwyn, Sask
July 9th 1935

Rt. Hon. R.B.Bennett

Dear Sir
    this is the first time in my life I have asked any one for help and I
came to the West in 1878 a baby with my parents I was only four
years, and saw many hard times as well as continual frights of the
Indians. our youngest boy, has just wrote off his grad 12, and wants
to be a dentist. which the farm can't afford to get him through. he
intends trying for a job, which is just as impossable, and as I heard of
so many kind acts you have done, I thought I would ask you, if you
would send me what money you could spare. I am not letting any
one know I am asking you for help.

Yours thankfully
Mrs Gerald McCord

[Reply: $4.00.]

399009

Regina, Sask.,
July 9/35.

Dear Mr. Bennett:

    Being an ardent supporter of you, I realize how busy you are, and
I realize I should not bother you with my troubles; but, having tried
earnestly elsewhere, and having failed, I turn to you.

    You have, no doubt, already surmised that I am seeking aid,
probably financial aid, from you. You are right. Let me state my
case briefly. I am a young girl of nineteen, of poor but honest
family, and of more than average ability. Just this summer, after a
long struggle and much sacrifice on the part of my parents, I have
succeeded in obtaining my B.A. I desire to teach, teaching seems
more than a "job" to me — for I earnestly believe I have the gift of
imparting knowledge, I believe teaching is my vocation. Accordingly,
I want to go to Saskatoon to obtain my Certificate of Education.
But we simply have not the money. I have no means of earning it,
and try as I may, I cannot borrow it. It is necessary for me to go this
Fall: for my parents need my help as soon as I can give it to them.
They are both too old to obtain work, my father is sixty-five and
crippled with rheumatism. They are near the breaking-point; their
sole hope is me, and I must hurry to help them. We have been on
relief; the small expenses at the small College I attended here have
been paid by an uncle. But the uncle is no longer in a position to
help me. And so, as a final hope, I come to you. I do not ask you to
give me the money; I ask to borrow it, and will give you a note for
it. I have acquaintances in Regina who will back my word should
you desire them to do so; men who are in public positions and
whose word you will accept if you would not accept mine. Or if you
should want references from which you could find out if I am truthfully stating my case, I can give them to you.

    You will not regret helping me; I am a good student and will
make the best of my opportunity given me. My uncle is proud that I
am a ward of his, and has never regretted helping me.

    I require $400. It is a large sum, but I promise to repay it, if you
lend it to me.

    I realise your position; an unknown girl is asking you for money,
and her letter may be full of lies. But I have tried to make my appeal
simple and sincere; and as I said before, I do not ask you to accept

my word only. But if you should consider my case, merely let me know, and I will immediately have men write you, whose word you will accept.

I need not add that I am a strong Conservative, and especially an ardent admirer of our premier; for if it were not so I would not have written this. I don't believe I could help being a Conservative, even if my reason dictated otherwise, it is in my blood.

And so, I place myself in your hands. Every other course has failed. Upon you alone rests the fulfilment of the desires of a young Canadian girl and the happiness of two lovely old people. If you help me, I promise you will not regret it.

At least, I beg of you, give me a reply, even if you deny me my request. I shall be praying to the dear Lord and awaiting a letter from you. If I appeal to you in His name, can you refuse me?

Yours hopefully,
L.E. Macdonald

P.S. Perhaps I should add that I have a Governor-General's medal to my credit, and have always passed my exams with high marks.

L.E.Macdonald

[Reply]

Personal and Confidential.
Ottawa, 13th July, 1935

Dear Miss Macdonald,—

I am today sending you this note in reply to your letter of the 9th instant, addressed to the Prime Minister.

Mr. Bennett receives an enormous number of appeals from students for assistance but, in spite of the fact that there are many names ahead of yours, he was so greatly impressed by the way you have written that he proposes to advance you the $400.00 which you require, in order that you may go to Saskatoon this fall.

Will you be good enough to let me know on what date you would like him to send you the money. He will advance $200.00 as a first payment, and the balance of $200.00 as required. On hearing from you, this matter will be given attention.

In view of the large number of appeals received by Mr. Bennett, will you be good enough to treat this matter as confidential.

Yours faithfully,
Secretary

[Reply]

Regina, Sask.,
July 26/35.

Dear Mr. Bennett:

I received your letter saying you had granted my request, and you have made me the happiest girl alive. My good fortune is almost unbelievable, and so great is my gratitude that I cannot express it in words. Let me say alone that I am intensely grateful and that I thank you with all my heart. I only hope I can someday do something for you, although it seems impossible to ever fully repay your kindness.

I will regard as sacred your wish that this matter be kept strictly confidential.

I have written the University, but as yet I have not received a reply. However, if you will be so kind as to advance $200. by Sept. 15, I'm sure that will be soon enough. I will keep you informed as to my progress at school, and I will let you know when I require the remainder of the money.

Thanking you again, sincerely,

I remain,
Yours gratefully,
Lorraine Macdonald

398972-7

Banff, Alta.
July 10, 1935

Government head office
Ottawa.

Dear Sir —
   I'm very bad need of help is there any help I can get. I have three
children and my husband is dead & I'm keeping house for a man in
banff and I get nothing much. I get little board, me & the children
very bad need of clothes. the man I'm keeping house for tells me to
take my children & go but I can't go any where when I have a peny
to my name & no clothes to wear. So will you please assist me and
my children.

Your very truly
Mrs. Ella Stone

[Reply: $5.00.]

398850

Magdalen Islands Quebec
July 19 1935

Honaurable mr Bennett
dear Sir you Will Excuse me but iam a Poor Woman 70 years old and
i have a sick husband and he is 71 and not abel to work and we have
no one to keep us and i heard you were a good kind gentelman to
the old and i thought i would Write and ask you if you could Please
send us a little money to get some coal and flower for one Winter
and We will do all we can in the coming Election the same as we

boath did in the last one so trusting to hear from you soon We
Remain your servants

Mr & Mrs
Jonathan A. Stewart

[Reply: $5.00.]

400029-30

Winnipeg, Manitoba
July 24th-1935

Dear Sir:—

I received your letter some days past and have also received a
letter from Mr. Sims of the Dominion Telegraphs. In his letter he
states that there are no openings at this time and will keep my letter
for further reference.

I have been waiting to hear from Hon. W.J.Major but have not
had a letter from him as yet.

Once again I must thank you for your inclosure it again came in
as handy if not handier than before, for the same use as mentioned
in my last letter.

Since my last writing we have been more unfortunate as two of
our children are now confined to the hospital with Whooping Cough.
They were very ill and were losing weigh very seriously and have had
to be taken to the hospital to be fed through their skin.

I have the offer of starting to work on the 1st of August for a
Power Company as a Lineman. This job is not an easy one but one
of climbing Steel towers, etc. The wages would be better than $8.00
per day and would be for 44 hours per week. But as usual there are
obstacles in my way. I have tried locally the past few days to secure
a loan of sufficient money to pay my way out to the job and enough
to secure tools which I have not. The *recent strikes* have made things
so that one must pay his way to get to a job as one cannot get there
now like a person could before. Therefore I have a fare of $14.00

and about $30.00 for tools to secure. But this amount is impossible
for me to raise. It figures out at one weeks wage that I must secure
to be able to get on the job. I have offered to return it at the end of
August but as I have been out of work so long all my collateral is
disolved and therefore my credit rating is below par.

I have had a fair amount of experience in this work and I am sure
that I could keep going on this job if I were able to get out on it.

However I am afraid that I am not going to get on it as I have
already mentioned that the possibility of my securing the necessary
finance before the end of this month are almost remote.

I am sure though that if I were in Ottawa at this time and able to
see Mr. Bennett that I would be successful in this venture.

If you could care to mention my case once again to your friend
whom knows Mr. W.J.Major I would appreciate knowing as I understand there is to be some work done this fall which I may be
successful in obtaining if your friend would care to assist me in
getting. It will be of temporary nature however and would be very
helpful in obtaining.

The other mentioned job would be good till possible the end of
March or April.

Thanking you for your assistance and consideration I will remain.

Yours very sincerely,
Charles Grierson

396082-4

[This handwritten note follows Charles Grierson's letter of July 24th
and concludes the file:]

R.K.F.

Would you ask Mr. Major if he has a job for father of 4. I do *not
recommend him* as I do not know him but we can give the
appearance of interest.

[See previous letters from Grierson on pp. 22, 46, 68, 151, 156, 161.]

Rollinstown Alta
Aug 6th 1935

Prime Minister R.B.Bennett

Dear Sir
  I am writing you to see if there is anything you would be kind enough to do towards finding me employment of a nature that I could do.
  I am a young man having lost a leg above the knee some fourteen years ago. I have been on direct relief for the past four years receiving the sum of ten dollars per month. I have written on numerous occasions to the supervisor of releif and the Deputy Minister of public works Edmonton begging to be given employment of a nature that I could do in preference to charity   They have been most courteous and sympathetic when replying to my applications but always stating they were very sorry indeed but they could not find me employment of any kind. While I appreciate the sympathy shown me, Sympathy alone can do but very little to alleviate one in my position
  Without the aid of charity this certainly would be a very cruel world on the other hand the bread of charity is very bitter indeed. I am in much need of a new limb at present time but have not the necessary means fitted with a good limb there are numerous jobs I could do and would willing do in order to get away from direct releif and the stigma attached to it I may state that I enjoy perfect health
  Anything you would be kind enough to do towards finding me work of any kind in order to be self supporting and be able to look into the future with confidence I certainly would appreciate it
  Inspector Thompson R.C.M.P. of Edmonton formly of Bandeath or Sargent Cawsey of Bandeath is very familiar with my position and

could outline my case. I can assure you that if given employment I will endeavor to give the utmost satisfaction

Yours Truly
Paul Henderson

[Reply: $5.00.]

400466-8

Braemore, Saskatchewan
Aug 10th 1935

Dear Mr. Bennett;
    As I can think of no one else whom I feel would more willingly aid us, I am coming to you, with a very personal little problem.
    When I tell you that our crops are a failure here again, this year, owing to rust, you will, I am sure, understand my motive in writing to you, personally.
    We, the Young people of the district would like to make our teacher a substantial present. He has been with us seven years, & is going to be married within the next two months, so everyone feels that he is worthy of something more than we can do. Our district is almost two thirds foreigners, & they do not seem very ready to help about doing anything.
    I want you to understand that any donation, however small, would be very gratefully received.

I am,
Very Sincerely Yours,
Mrs. B.A.Trainer

[Reply: $5.00.]

398858

Marshall Alta.
Aug. 14. 1935

Dear Hon. Premier R.B.Bennett.
I am an invalid. I have T.B. of the kidney and bladder. I was at
the Marshall Hospital for 3½ months. have been in bed at home now
for 4 months I am improving, but in 2 weeks, I have to go back to
hospital again to have another Xray picture taken, and a course of
treatment, and the Picture and medicine are cash. and we have know
money for it. And I am applying to you for help. I do not know of
any one else to apply to. I have know relatives that can help me.
We have not had a crop for 4 years and our crop this year is poor
due to draught. I am a middle aged woman with 3 children. are old
timers of Alberta. I need help now more than ever before to fight
my sickness, or else die.
The municipality say they have enough with the relief problem. A
check for $100. or 75 dollars is like a drop in the ocean for the
Government, while to me it might mean Health and Happiness again.
So Hoping and praying that you will help me with a little money. I
am interested in all your doings. These statements are all true. I
would not beg for help if I was well, but I must have medicine. So
Please if you can send me a check soon big or small. And you shall
be Blessed and always remembered. I wish this to be confidential.
Thanking you in advance, I am,

Mrs. T.H. Olson

P.S. I do not wish this to be made public. I have Pride, but up
against it for money now for my Doctoring.

[Reply: $5.00.]

398779-80

Aug 1935
Renfrew Ont.

Mr Bennett

Dear Sir & Friend
Just a line to see if there is eny thing for me in this My Daughter & I
both ware confined at the same time She being 24 yrs & I 43 at the
time of their birth we ware living at Birks falls Ont at the time We
both ware in the same house & had the same Dr & nurce & Just 15
munits between their birth My Daughter was home on a visit at the
time she & her husband & 2 other children ware living at Rondeau
Park then, the children will be 10 years old on the 17th Dec they are
both fair & the same size & in the same book at School we are all
living in Renfrew if you would like their picture I could get one
taking & send one to you now this is personal & if you see fit to
answer this dont let the Donenes* get all the prase. My children are
in bad need of close for winter ware, I have the Mothers allounce
there are 4 of us 2 girls, & myself & my husband he is not able to
work My girl past in to first form & I havent the money to buy her
books & she needs a coat for winter My alounce is 35 a month

Yours Truly
Mrs Mary Watson

We are all conservets

[*Apparently a reference to the Dionne quintuplets.]

[Reply: $5.00.]

398396-7

Cantal Sask
Aug 15/35

Mr. Bennett   I am a Mother left with a little girl 1 year old, and I
have nothing, and I am badly in need and unable to work
     And as Winter is coming on, and my baby needs everything, I
have no warm cloths either, but I think of my baby first.
     I was told you would help, so I thought I would write for babys
sake. Mr. Bennett I'd be very grateful if you could send me some
money

Yours Very Truly
Ellen Field

[Reply: $5.00.]

398860

Mouse Mountain, Alta, Can.
Aug 16th, 1935

Dear Gentleman:
     I am writing a letter to you, explaining to you some of my dread-
ful misfortunes. I think its' a matter of consideration, and I would
like to beg you to help me in some way. As now the times are hard, I
cannot make a living in any way. Being in a poor state, my family
being all helpless, another baleful misfortune has occured. On
August thirteenth my house burned down, due to the strikening of
the lightning. Also the things that have been inside the house have
burned down too. Now as I want to put up a knew house I cannot
get lumber for time, because I have debts in many other places. So
now I live in the old granery. As winter is drawing nigh I don't know
how I am ever going to get through it. Just recently on August
fifteenth we had a heavy frost here and ruined my crop. Now there
is no possible way of making a living whatsoever. Therefore I am
floundering about in the dark being in a tremendous loss. As you see

in what a state I am now. I'd like you to help me in some way
another. But if you do help me I will never foreget you till the last
day of my life. Please answer soon.

Yours very truly,
Ken Prandyk

398862-5

Bruceville, Ont.
Aug. 24, 1935

Rt. Hon. R.B.Bennett
Ottawa Canada

Dear Sir.
    On July 21st we engaged a transient for a month to work on the
farm. He finished his month on Thursday morning and we even
drove him to the station as he said he was going to Cornwall.
Thursday night we were invited to a wedding about two and one
half miles from home. On Friday we discovered several things
missing. A mens gold watch and chain, a ladies white gold wrist
watch, two sums of money, 2 shirts, razor, and two suits of clothes.
We arc sure it was the transient as I always kept small change in the
oven of the stove. Just for convenience, (the stove not being used in
summer). I mention this to show the gratitude the farmer receives
from using these fellows decently. We are a struggling farm family
and are trying to educate children. We have a son that we are sending
to McGill & working under difficulties. The two suits stolen belong
to him. I was trying to scrape up enough money to get him a new
one before University opened and now he hasn't a suit to leave the
farm. Nothing left but overalls. I know you would not miss twenty-
five or fifty dollars to help get this boy clothes. This is no sham
story. We are all well acquainted with the Stormont member. Mr.
Frank Shaver, attending the same church so he can vouch for

honesty of this plea. Hoping you will be able to help in this. I
remain.

Yours truly,
Mrs. Seymor R. Plunkett

398873-4

Ardath, Sask.
Aug. 24/35

Dear Mr. Bennett,
    I have heard mamma and daddy talk about you so much, and
what a good man you are. I am a little boy eight years old and I'm in
Grade III at school. I've wanted a little red wagon to hich my dog to
for so many years, but daddy has no money. Please, Mr. Bennett
would you send me enuff money to buy my wagon. Thank you so
much.

Your very good friend,
Horace Gardiner

398534

Ardath Sask
Aug 31/35

Dear Mr. Bennett,
    Thanks very much for the money. I'm going to get the wagon.
Mamma said I could.

Your friend,
Horace Gardiner

P.S. I am going to vote for you when I get to a big boy.

Your friend,
Horace Gardiner

398538-9

Ottawa, Ontario.
August 30, 1935

Rt. Honourable R.B.Bennett.
Prime Minister of Canada.
Chateau Laurier.

Rt. Honourable Sir:
   It is perhaps a very unusual thing for you to receive correspondence of this nature, and especially from one who is unknown
heretofore by you. I sincerely trust that the lack of formality will be
understood and will in no way fail to bring a desired answer to the
request contained herein.
   I am not ignorant that, as Canada's leading statesman, you have
business of a most important nature. Yet, this letter concerns the
business of the *King of Kings,* and since "the King's business
requireth haste" (I Sam. 21:8), I am making known to you my part
in this great enterprize.
   I was born in the village of Edward on November 18, 1911 of
good, nominal Christian parents. In all, there were 9 children born in
our family. From childhood we were brought up in the way of
righteousness, and my parents saw to it that we attend both Church
and Sabbath School. This has all been a blessing to me in my young
life and I shall never cease to thank God for such thoughtful parents.
   On July 16, 1928 I said "Good-Bye" to home and loved ones and
set out to face the World. The Lord had His hand on my life from
the very outset and in May 1929 I was converted to God by the
regenerating power of God's Holy Spirit according to St. John's

Gospel, Chapter 3. My life, since that time, has not ceased to tell for the Christ whom I love and adore. Yet, He loved me before I loved Him.

Believing that He was calling me to the Christian Ministry, I resigned my position with the Sun Life Insurance Company one year ago August 31. I entered the Moody Bible Institute in Chicago in September 1934 and remained there until the Christmas vacation in December. Returning to Canada I was then unable to resume my studies due to financial difficulties. Employment seemed out of the question and as a result I have worked only 7 weeks in the last eight months. I feel that God would have me continue my studies and I am ready to go into this large field of service. I am interested in a Canadian Institute of the Free Methodist Church at Lorne Park, Port Credit, Ontario. This college offers a 4 year course, which I feel I can reduce to 3 years due to my High School Education. There are opportunities for the students to partially defray expenses, but a substantial sum of money is needed to start. All the books and clothing have to be purchased as well as an amount each month to cover the cost of room, board & tuition. Mr. D.L.Moody, one of America's foremost Evangelists of the last Century believed that God's needy servants had the privilege of telling the Lord, as well as God's people the need of the work. I am convinced, through what I have heard and read in the local newspapers that I am addressing one who is a follower of the Lord Jesus Christ. Believing this to be the case I have every confidence that I have secured your interest in the work of the Master along this line.

The expenses at Lorne Park College are not unreasonable. The board, room, and tuition amount to about $30.00 per month. There are 10 months to each school year. As I have intimated before, there are always opportunities given to work part time on the Institute Farm to defray part of the expense, and I propose to buy up every opportunity.

With reference to my character, for I feel that I am unknown to you, I might refer you to the following Christian gentlemen by whom I am well known in this city:

Mr. F.C.Blair — Ass't. Deputy-Minister of Immigration —
Sergeant Alexander Fraser of the R.C.M.Police —
Rev. Andrew Telford — Pastor of the Metropolitan Tabernacle —
Rev. C.B.Smith, Pastor of Bethel Pentecostal Tabernacle —

With reference to political standing I might say that I am a staunch supporter of the Conservative Party, and my family before me have always stood firm for the policies of the Conservative Government.

I trust that I have not imposed upon you, Honourable Sir, but that as a child of God you will readily understand the situation.

I beg to remain, Sir,

Your obedient Servant,
In Christ
Gordon J. Evans

[Reply]

Personal
Ottawa, September 5, 1935.

Dear Mr. Evans:

I must thank you for having written me so very excellent a communication as that which I received a few days ago.

It is clear to me that you have your heart in the work in which you are engaged and that you should find an opportunity to complete your studies in the way in which you indicate, but just now I am in a position which makes it impossible for me to assist you. There are seven or eight young people at colleges and schools, whose expenses I am defraying, and the last one, which I undertook only a few days ago, exhausts all the money I have available for that purpose this year.

However, I see that you require at least three hundred dollars and, if a couple of your friends will give you a hundred dollars each, notwithstanding the fact that I have exhausted my funds for that purpose, I will try and find the other hundred for you, because of

the earnestness of your desire to be a Minister and to serve the
cause of your Master.

   With all good wishes, believe me, I am,

Yours faithfully,
R.B.Bennett

400108-12

Ruthven, Ont.
Sept. 1935

The Honourable R.B.Bennett, Ottawa Ont.

Dear Sir:—
   It is with pleasure I write you to-day But you will be surprised to
hear from such a small boy as me. I am geting an adult to write it for
me. For I am just 7 yrs old probably you won't take time to read my
wee letter. But however I have had a terrible experience in my short
lifetime I am eight yrs old on the 14 day October which is election
day and I was wondering if you could give me some help to be able
to attend school & walk once more. By supplying me with an
artificial leg. My leg was shot off last November with a shot gun at
close range with a boy who picked it up in another house. I wasn't
expected to live atall. But I am here to-day. But 7th July I fell &
broke my sore leg on the kitchen floor so was back in the hospital
again I spent Xmas in the hospital was there a long time too. My Dad
& Mother are staunch supporters of the Conservative Party, & so are
all the Bancrofts. I am active & well every other way so when I play I
often get hurt, if I just had a leg I could go back to school I am in Sr
1st Book if you don't beleive my history just ask Dr Shellington of
Windsor he took off my leg along with Dr Metcalfe of Kingsville he
is my Doctor. If you will say you will help me a little, I will send
you my phota. We live on a farm a rough one havn't been able to
pay our interest for 2 years now & principal the same., so you understand our circumstances. Probably you will be able to get me an

artificial limb for my birthday the 14th day of October so as my
people will feel like going out to vote that day. The price of my leg
would probly mean alot for a fellow when the judgement day comes
I know there are many other little crippled boys & girls too But I
feel if I had my leg I would be able to help some poor Robin back in
his nest again. Now Would you like me to send you my picture I will
do so. Hoping you will be so kind to give me the price of an artificial
leg or pay for it when I get it, as we can't affort it & it maybe joy in
the skies for you. I know you will answer my letter

Yours Very Truly
Master George Bancroft

398635-7

[Newspaper clipping]

DEPRESSION FACTOR

The death of James C. Grant, 22, *unemployed bookkeeper,* and member of the Toronto Flying Club, who
jumped 1,500 feet from the wing of an aeroplane Saturday evening after bidding a smiling farewell to his in-
structor, Flight Lieutenant Ralph Spradbrow ...

Hon. R.B.Bennett
I would say the Dominion Government was the murderer of this
young Canadian, in that it is in their power to do something for the
unemployed, but have not done so.

Leo Gadali
Toronto

486834

Calgary Alta
Sept 3rd 1935

Dear Mr. Bennett
    I dont know weather you will think worth while to take any
notice of this or not. But when a person is in a desperate situation
they are apt to do some funny things that they wouldnt think of
under ordanary circumstances. I have been thinking over this idea of
writing to you for three days before I summoned up enough courage
to do so. I think you know who I am. I am the second son of Mr
J.C.P.Manzer of Halifax N.S. and have been in Alberta about 40
years. I was 64 years old last May. I have managed to make a living
up to about a month ago. The last seven years I have been working
for Mr R.C.Jonas as a night elevator man at the old Jonas Apart-
ments and the Hotel Wellington in Calgary, but the first week in
August I was discarged. For the last five years I have been receiving
$50 dollars a month wages for my wife and myself to live on.
    We even helped my oldest daughter a little out of that as she is on
munisapal relief, and has been for about three years. she has four
children to feed, and the relief they get is very little.
    Of course I had to apply for relief right away after being dis-
charged, as I hadnt a cent to live on. But I also made application for
a soldier's allowance. as I am a returned man. I asked if they would
give anything for the loss of our boy. Our only boy was killed in
active service on the Battle field. They said no they couldnt. They
seem to like to try to give a lot of trouble in getting this allowance. I
had to send to Halifax for my Birth certificate. then after two or
three day's after I thought that they had sent the papers to Ottawa I
received a note from the Calgary Office, asking for my Marriage
certificate. Well I couldnt give them the origanal certificate as it was
lost or destroyed in some way in moving around so much. so I gave
them a copy of it that my wife sent down east to Lockport N.S.
where we were married on the 28th of December 1892 but when I
handed it to them they said it wasnt any good as it hadnt and stamp
or seal on it to show that it was genuine. Well I said it answered all
right for my wife in 1916 while I was overseas. And the City relief
Officials thought it was all right. If it answered the purpose on
two other occasions why shouldnt it this time. Well they said they
would send it for what it was worth but they didnt think it would

do for the Officials at Ottawa. Now my aim in writing this letter is that I thought you might be kind enough to do me a favor of either phoning or write a short note to the department Officials at Ottawa that look after that kind of thing. and recomend my case to them to put it through without any more trouble. I was told that it would be $40 for us $20 for my wife and $20. for myself. My youngest Daughter lives in Nanaimo on Vancouver Island. and we hear from her about every two weeks, and in nearly every letter we receive from her she begs us to try and come there to live, as we could manage to live much cheaper than we can in Calgary. She is married and has two children one 10 years old the other 6 years. before leaving Calgary they were on the City relief, for quite a while and sinse going to Nanaimo they have managed to live, or exist I should say. and have managed to buy a small lot of ground and build a little house of their own sinse going there two years ago. without haveing any help from the town. She thinks if we could manage to get a small peice of land so as to grow our own vegetables that we could live quite comfortable on the allowance that we would get. Well I had better stop. I guess you think this a queer letter. but as the saying goes, a drowning person will grasp for a straw. so this is like the last straw with me but hoping it is something more substantial than a straw, I remain your

Admiring Friend
Frank E. Manzer

84007-11

Blaine Lake, Sask.
Sept. 9, 1935

Hon. R.B.Bennett
Ottawa, Ont.

Dear Sir:—

For some time I have been thinking what this new country of ours was coming to. I had the pleasure of talking with Mr. F.R. MacMillan M.P. of Saskatoon and Senator Hornor of Blaine Lake. They both insisted that I write you a line.

I wish to give my opinion of relief. First it is a shame for a strong young man to ask for relief in this country. To my mind the relief has helped out the C.C.F. and Social Credit. When you give an inch they take a foot. There are men, who have been on relief, now sitting on the street asking $2.50 and 3.00 per day Many of them would not be worth a $1.00 per day to stook 60 ct. wheat.

To my mind the poet is right nine times out of ten. The best thing that can happen to a young man is toss him overboard and compel him to sink or swim, in all my acquaintance I have never known one to drown who was worth saving.

When I hear young men, with their head full of book knowledge, complaining about no money no work. They say they'll try for relief and they get it, then they spend two or three months around a lake shore rolling in the sand and splashing in the water. When winter comes they have no preparations of any kind They say they'll try for relief and they get it.

I say again a man must have a purpose in life if he hasn't he will never amount to much. He will eat that which he has not earned, he will clog the wheels of industry and stand in the way of progress. Thoughts of this kind should be empressed on the pupils by the teachers, and ministers, instead of the C.C.F. doctrine, and athletic sports. The people have gone silly over nonsense and it is our leaders that are teaching the younger generations to be useless.

I asked a young man to help me thresh, he said he would not pitch sheaves for less than $5.00 per day, he can get relief, no doubt. I have four young men four harvest and threshing, they blow their wages every Saturday night, some of them will be on relief this winter, if not all.

It takes hardship to make real men and women so cut out relief, and get rid of such men as Peter Verigan,* Tim Buck and Evans.†

Relief is like a sixteen year old boy getting money from dad, when the old man gets wise and tightens up the boy gets mad and cuts a shine just as the relief strikers did.

There are some people in this country who are in hard circumstances, but I can safely say there is no one having the hardships that we pioneers had 28 and 30 years ago.

Yours turely
L.M.Himmer

[*Peter Chistiakov Vergirin ('Peter the Purger') was a radical Doukhobor leader; in constant legal difficulties, he received nation-wide attention as a result of the federal government's attempt to deport him to Russia in 1933.]

[†Arthur H. Evans: Communist leader of striking relief camp workers whose 'march' to Ottawa ended in rioting and bloodshed in Regina on July 1, 1935. In June Evans had repeatedly called Bennett a liar during the course of an interview with the Prime Minister.]

489865-8

Timmins Ont
Sept 25, 1935

Sir
I am writing to ask you if you would kindly help my family and i we really need it i have written to Hepburn and Croll and Roebuck* and none of them will do any thing my husband has money and he will not buy clothes or feed as right he has been in jail twice for abusing me and also the children i wish you could send a Health inspector hear the bed are in a awful state the *children have no clothes warm enough to go 1½ to school* and i have had 14 children in 23 years 2 are dead have a boy 21 years of age will not help me I took 4 years

to get him on the mines he promise to give me 25 dollars a month to help his sisters and Brothers now he has the job he will not give a cent the youngest is 2 years old we have not one blanket on the bed only old coats and quilts the judge hear when i put a summons in for my husband he and the Provincle Police Dexter fixes it in court and he does not even have to go and see the court house I have had warrants made and he has changed them to summons when I told Dexter about it he laugh at me but it is the truth Sir Judge Robert-son there is no law with him at all Judge Chapleau is a good true judge to all people Sir he see both sides of the story and give them what they need my husband made 500 Dollars this summer with 3 children selling vegetables i went 2½ weeks too and he has about 1,000 hid around the house and we have not a shirt or under wear to put on he owes all the doctors in town and will not pay the hospital and told me i can tell who I like but let them find it he steal tools when he work on releif last winter I told Hepburn he takes no notice at all and will do nothing to help will not answer the letter i write Sir

Mrs. Agnes Kenston

[*At that time Hepburn, Croll, and Roebuck were, respectively, premier, minister of welfare, minister of labour, in Ontario.]

398722-3

St Theobald Que
Sept.-27, 1935

Mr. Hon. R.B.Bennett

Dear Sir
I suppose you will think its an auful thing of me writing you this letter but its hard time that makes me do it I did not get a days work since the last five years I lost my job the first day after the last Alection they told me that I had voted for Mr Bennett, and they would not give me any more work so I done nothing since that time

that amount to any thing so this is why I writing to you to see if you could help me now I am in a bad shape I got cripple last winter and will not be able to work for a long time and have a big family to keep I am sure I have lost at least one dollar a day since I voted for the Bennett Government but if I can get some thing for what I lost, now that I need it I will vote for your Government at the next election same as I done the last time. So if you can help me before the next election that will be 50 or 60 votes more for you hoping to from you before the election

Yours Truly
Maurice Cormier

400204-5

Dearborn Man
September 27,/35

Dear Sir:
    I hate doing such a thing as this, but I really have to. I would like you to help me. I havent got any place of my own. I am not feeling well, and am not working any place. I am 67 years old. So you know it is hard. I have children going to school. They have to go 3 miles to school, and in mud & water up to their knees. They have no rubbers, nor shoes. They have no winter clothes. They only have a few light rags to wear.
    We had no grain, nor garden Everything was drown out. I don't know how I'll live the winter.

Please help me. If you do help me. Then I'll help you. Please help
with clothing other things.

Yours Truly
Mr. Geo. Kryzaniwsky

[Reply: $5.00.]

400531

Ayr Ontario
Oct 1 1935

Mr Bennett

Dear Friend
I have been a good Conservative all my life. I am having a hard time
of it I got Gored with the Bull and my shoulder broken and my right
lung Ripped. I was a long time in the Galt Hospital and a large Bill to
Pay. I got behind with my taxes and Interest and I dont want to
loose my home. I think the Conservative Party *ought to try and help*
me out in some way. last fall I was short of feed with the dry season
and the reforme Party sent the Humane society after me and I lost
all my cattle they Just gave me to hours to get them off the Place or
they would take Charge of them. I just had to sacrifice them to
make sale I got a cent a pound for them. I haven't a Cow or a Pig on
the How do they expect I am going to live when I am deprived of
every thing to make a dollar out of I think this is all this time and I
sincerely wish you luck on Election day. from you Friend

George Holland

[Reply: $5.00.]

400444-6

New Liskeard, Ont
Oct 2 1931

Premier Bennette present canda.

Dear sir i am righting these few lines to tell you that i am a con-
servite and and i cant get a job on — post ofice that is Building in
New Liskeard. i live hear and have a family to suport   the most of
the men that are working on this post oface are outside men and us
men Beloning to this town cant get a days wurk   i think it a shame
to for men to be yoused like that and i have Been Out of work the
most of last year and this year all so i cant pay my taxes   i see
where my farm will Be sold for taxes   so if you want my vote the
next Electon you will have to Do More for me than you have up to
the present time   i now one thing if i lose my farm for taxes i sure
will never cast a nother vote for this government so if you want me
to give you my vote a gain i will aske you to send me nof money to
pay my taxes and that 1 Hundred and 20 Dollars is my taxes for lots
in town ship — i live in town at present But i want to go Back on my
farm again   you now i and my wife worked hard last Elicton we got
1 hundred and 11 vots for you   i am a Polish canadian and all those
vots that i got for you were polish people   i am willing to work for
you again if you help me in what i menchend and help me to get
work so i can suport my famly   i am a father of 6 childrens so
please let me now By return mail please   Be so kind and i will help
you a gain when the time comes a gain. i am a captner By trade

yours very truly,
Mr. A. Kesicki

394438-40

McAlpine, Ont.
Oct. 3, 1935

Dear Sir;—
   Droping you a line to *ask you for a little charity*. I have neither a
father or a mother my husband only has work in summertime I have
a poor little girl Three Years of age with hardly no cloths fit for the
cold, and myself being an expectant mother for New Years I have
got lots of worry as we havn't been able yet to save enough to pay
the doctor I had for the one Three Years old. Some of the neigh-
bours have been very good to give me cloths if times stays like this I
will have to place my two children and go to work. I thought mabe
that *you could* send me *a little* charity even if *its only* $1.00 or 50¢ I
would be very much Obliged. And if I can help you in any election I
surly will.

Yours Truly.
Mrs Hubert Provost

[Reply: $5.00.]

398735

Moose Lake, Manitoba
Oct. 3, 1935

Rt. Hon. R.B.Bennett
Ottawa, Ont.

Dear Sir,—
   As my pen traces your name upon the paper, I marvel at my
boldness in addressing you, the world's greatest statesman, a born
leader of the people, a stirring orator. Yet as I know you, the world's
riches do not tempt you and to help your needy people seems to be
the aim of your life.
   The night you spoke in Brandon, I wished that I could have heard

you, but lack of fare prevented me from going and I have not even
the radio to tune in and listen.

I heard you said that earthly wealth had no enticements for you
and I wondered there if out of your fullness you could spare an
humble follower what would redeem our small home from sale for
taxes. Four lean years of weary struggling, keeping ourselves off the
relief list but unable to keep up the taxes.

So I am asking you for Two hundred dollars to clear the debt and
keep our home. Wife of a man whose body is wasting with an in-
curable disease yet trying to fight life's battle, I ask this to be the
crowning act of five years and the beginning of another term of
office.

Please, I ask, do not put my letter in print or mention it; I trust
you will not.

One of your people.
Mrs. L.S.Stern

398562-3

Port Helen, Ontario
Oct. 3/1935

Dear Mr. Bennett.
Just a line to see if you would kindly aid us in our need of help. We
are living in a shack 18 x 14 ft. which is nothing but a burned shell.
Some time ago we had a fire and it burned everything we had. The
fire was put out in time that it did not burn the shack down. My
little home is cold as it has no windows just some places where there
is tin nailed up to keep out the biting cold. My husband is working
hard on relief trying to make a living for me and my five little
babies. I have five children all small and are not dressed warm. They
all have a cold now from not being properly dressed. My husband is
unable to buy clothes for them as he gets only three days a week on
relief. Some time this does not provide enough food for us all. Me
and my husband are conservative and always have been and always

will be. Would you please be so kind as to help us out. as cold
weather is coming on and I would like to build my tiny home a little
warmer to provide room for us all. I have two little girls that are
school age and are unable to go to school being not dressed warm
enough. The school authorities are after me to send my children to
school. I sent them to school two weeks ago and to-day they are sick
and can't go. My husband has been out trying his best to help you to
get all the votes you can. Nearly everyone in our neighborhood have
turned conservative as my husband spends many tireless hours
talking to them of what all you have done for them. Will you kindly
answer my letter soon as I would like to hear from you the coming
week.

    And kindly oblige

Yours truly
Mrs Leslie Horne

400423-4

Ecum Secum Oct 4th 1935

Premier R.B.Beinnett

Dear Sir
I am writing you a few lines to see if you can help me out to get
some food and clothing I am left a widow now over a year ago My
Husband died in Halifax in H.G.Hospital with kidney trouble and
now I have no support now I use to work years ago in Labiters
Factory But now my hands are crippled with Reumitism and I is not
able to work. So you see I am destitute of clothes and food and we
have voted on your side ever since, I had a vote and it is ten votes
rite around me is on your side and it was no Employment on the
roads for anyone this sumer and I heard they were giving the *old age
pensions* from Sixty now and I am nearly 65 and I want you to try
and preceed to see if you can get it for me as I am in need very much
for we have done our very best to keep you in and we will continue

on and try if you can get some help for me I heard you would look after the poor people. So please answer my letter and tell me all about it

Yours truely
Mrs Jeremy Humboldt

Please answer rite soon

[Reply: $5.00.]

398739-40

Goulden Ont
Oct 7

Dear Mr Bennet,
    I suppose your busy so close to eliction day. My mamma is goung to vote for your side. I am alittle girl eight years old and am in 3rd class but I haven't any coat to wear to school those cold mornings and mamma can't buy me one we haven't any money I'd be glad of any little you could send me I hope your succesful in the election your lovinly

Valerie Dickinson

[Reply: $2.00.]

400214

Whiteway N.B.
Oct 7. 1935

Right Hon. R.B.Bennett,

Dear Sir: —
I am writing to ask you if you could or would help me. As I have
a big family and all are going to school at present, but I will soon
have to keep them home as they have no clothes and very little to
eat I have been working nearly all summer but my pay was so small
that I barley got enough eat for them. There are six children, ages
from 15 to 7, four of which are boys, one boy 13, and in Grade
VIII. I would like for him to be in school till he get through. But
with out help of some kind, I can't. I try every way to get work.
There is no work and wages so small. All I can do is to get something
to eat for my wife and children, and so many school books to buy,
besides three of our children have one book between them. No way
of getting any more The times have been so hard around here that
everything one had is all worn out. This very night we havn't a
baking of flour in our house. I have order some whether we will get
it I can't tell. No work nor no money I think it is a terrible thing for
a man that is able and willing to work he has to see his little children
go to school hungry and half enough cloth on them to keep them
warm. I always support the Conservative Goverment, and intend to
do the same next Monday if nothing happen.
    I don't mind my self so bad. the children I am thinking most of
now. I don't know How I am going to get cloth for them if your
help me I would be very thankful to you.
    I remain Your Truly,

Bruce Bass

[Reply: $5.00.]

398576-8

Hon. R.B.Bennett
Ottawa

Sir:—

This is from a mother who's son is wandering somewhere in Ont.
trying vainly to get work. What are you going to do for these
thousands of young men? There is lots of work to be done if you
would only start them at it. You have never had to sleep out in the
snow and rain or go days without food. Just stop and think of these
hungry boys when you are at your next banquet.

You have no children, so you cannot realize how parents feel
with their sons wandering in this useless search for work.

You have only a short time now to try to help these men or it
will be up to the other party to do it.

A Mother

487006